Endorsements

Author Renae Brumbaugh Green enjoys her real-life romantic comedy life or endures it (depending on how much coffee she's had)! Her latest book, *Latte for Life: Ruth*, inspires us to see how the almost fairy-tale yet true account of Ruth and Boaz is similar to our own love story with the Prince of Peace—complete with happy ending. If you love Rom-Coms, coffee, grinning, and Jesus, this book's for you.

—KATHY CARLTON WILLIS, speaker, women's ministry director, and multi-book author, including *Grin with Grace*

Author Renae Brumbaugh Green has penned a book that mirrors her tender and committed heart. A deeply devoted woman of God, Renae brings spiritual truth to the surface in a way that enables women everywhere to relate and apply that truth. These short but powerful readings will bless and change your life!

—KATHI MACIAS (www.kathimacias.com), best-selling author of more than fifty books, including the 2011 Golden Scrolls Novel of the Year, *Red Ink*

Latte for Life is a heavenly brew of wisdom and wit. You will discover how to drink deeply of God's presence, and you will come away inspired and invigorated for another day. Highly recommended!

—ANITA HIGMAN, award-winning author of more than forty books

LATTE
for
LIFE

45 Devotions
from the book
of RUTH

Renae Brumbaugh Green

BroadStreet
P U B L I S H I N G

BroadStreet Publishing Group, LLCw
Racine, Wisconsin, USA
BroadStreetPublishing.com

LATTE for LIFE: 45 Devotions from the Book of RUTH

Copyright © 2016 Renae Brumbaugh Green

ISBN-13: 978-1-4245-5366-2 (hardcover)
ISBN-13: 978-1-4245-5367-9 (e-book)

Stock or custom editions of BroadStreet Publishing titles may be purchased in bulk for educational, business, ministry, fundraising, or sales promotional use. For information, please e-mail info@broadstreetpublishing.com.

Cover design by Chris Garborg at GarborgDesign.com
Interior by Katherine Lloyd at theDESKonline.com

Printed in China
16 17 18 19 20 5 4 3 2 1

Contents

Foreword

I usually don't find Christian literature very interesting, but by some sort of divine arrangement, I was invited by the author to write this foreword. From the moment I started reviewing *Latte for Life*, I could not drop it because of the combination of humor and the use of Disneyland fairy stories to explain Scriptures in the most simplistic, fascinating, and straightforward manner that I have ever come across. This devotional got me glued to the few chapters I was privileged to read.

The structure and the style of writing allows for easy reading and understanding, even for the younger generation who may be like some of us—not patient enough, finding some books too academic or boring. But Green's writing is the complete opposite, as it is not only entertaining but stimulating, stirring up the inner being and opening the eyes of our understanding.

Latte is coffee, a beverage to be enjoyed or a stimulant to keep one alert. Like its coffee namesake, *Latte for Life* is both enjoyable and stimulating. The author uses the step-by-step approach of making and taking coffee, with cream and sugar for smoothness and sweetness, with an extra serving of a second cup, to the last drop. Verse by verse, Renae Brumbaugh Green gives an excellent narrative of the story of Ruth and brings the Scripture to life.

As a writer and teacher of the Word, Renae gives a good account and representation of the life of Ruth even before she was married into the family of Elimelech, through the period of the marriage, and after she became a widow. The reader is brought to an understanding of what led to God's favor upon Ruth—to have been the great-grandmother of King David—and subsequently to the birth of Jesus Christ our Lord.

It is said by our people in Africa, that in humor the truth of a situation can be ascertained. *Latte for Life* captures that very essence, describing what we like to call "from grace to grass" (but here aptly put as treasure to trash). The readings address everything from the meaning of legacy, to the role of a mother-in-law, the benefits of pledging allegiance, to having a good name and doing things right. The book of Ruth encourages us to live life as a true love story, and Renae helps us understand the bigger picture that is always present with the things of God.

I strongly recommend *Latte for Life: Ruth* to everyone, as it explains how our actions or inactions can bring about blessings or curses to us and even to those around us, and possibly to generations unborn, even to the complete wipe-out of a family lineage. It also gives understanding to those who are either having challenges or always in a hurry to make life-changing decisions due to temporary situations. Finally, this book allows people to truly appreciate who they are and what is expected of them under a God-ordained covering.

Blessings!

—His Royal Majesty Oba Dokun Thompson

The Oloni of Eti-Oni, Osun State; the first traditional ruler in Nigeria to be installed in the Church according to the Scriptures by the pouring of oil

Fairy Tale

Do you remember the story of the Frog Prince? The poor frog had the chore of trying to get the princess to fall in love with him. Or at least, she had to kiss him. It was easy for *him* to love *her*. She was beautiful, pure, and sweet. But the frog? He was ugly. He had slimy skin and a croaky, raspy voice. Why in the world would she love him?

But in the end, she did. In Disney's version of the popular fairy tale, the story gets turned around a bit. The coveted kiss turned the girl into a frog, but eventually it all worked out. The prince's love for her turned her into a princess, and they lived happily ever after.

I wonder if Ruth felt like the frog in that story. In her homeland, she was considered quite a catch. But when she found herself in the land of God's chosen ones, she was an outcast. A foreigner. Her skin was dark; her hair was coarse. She spoke with a funny accent. In this land, she was a frog with no hope for anyone to love her.

Yet unlike the frog in the story, Ruth didn't depend on trickery or magic to win her prince. Boaz saw Ruth and thought she was beautiful. He fell in love. He pursued her, cared for her, and brought her special gifts. In the end, he paid a high price to make her his bride. Boaz was a wealthy bachelor, a prince among men. Surely he could have had any woman he wanted, but he chose Ruth.

Many days, I feel like that frog—croaks and all. You certainly don't have to look very far to find my faults; they are right on the surface. Why would a prince ever want me?

Yet the Prince of Peace does. Like Boaz, He looked at me and fell in love. He pursued me. He cares for me and gives me special blessings. He even paid a very high price to make me His own. He gave His life for me.

The story of Ruth has a fairy-tale-like quality about it. The wealthy bachelor fell in love with the poor widow. He pursued her. He rescued her and they lived happily ever after. They had children and grandchildren and great-grandchildren, until one night, many generations later, one of their descendants named Mary gave birth to the true Prince. But the really great thing is, this isn't a fairy tale! It's a true story.

Thank you for choosing to go on this journey with me—a journey of love and romance and happily-ever-after. Fire up your coffee pot, add your freshly ground beans, and grab your favorite creamer. Here is what you can expect in the coming pages:

1. ***God's Word Says:*** This is a verse-by-verse study of Ruth, so each entry begins with Scripture.

2. ***First Cup:*** Like that delicious first taste of coffee in the morning, this section includes life-infusing commentary about the passage.

3. ***Cream and Sugar:*** Just as that flavored creamer adds sweetness and enhances our coffee experi-

ence, daily reflection and conversation with God enhances and sweetens our lives.

4. ***Second Cup:*** A great cup of coffee leaves us wanting a little more, and God's Word, when studied consistently, leaves us craving more of Him as well. This section provides a few more relevant Scriptures as food for thought.

5. ***The Last Drop:*** A pithy quote, to be savored like that last drop of coffee.

I wonder if God included this story in His Book just for fairy tale lovers like me. I suppose so, for He wanted me—and you—to know that sacrificial love and happy endings aren't always fictional. He has already written a beautiful love story for each of His children. All we have to do is accept His love, and the story will be about us. And one day, we will live our happily-ever-after for all eternity with the King of Kings.

1

TREASURE TO TRASH

God's Word Says

In the days when the judges ruled, there was a famine in the land, and a certain man of Bethlehem in Judah went to live in the country of Moab, he and his wife and two sons. (Ruth 1:1 NRSV)

First Cup

This first verse of Ruth is kind of like a news report. It tells the who, what, when, and where. The days of the judges were dark times in Israel's history. Israel had been led out of Egypt and into the Promised Land. You'd think they would live in gratitude to God for rescuing them, but think again. During this time, the Israelites pretty much did whatever they wanted and left God out of the picture. Sounds familiar, doesn't it?

This verse becomes even more interesting when we understand the meaning of some of the names. In Hebrew, Bethlehem means "house of bread" and Judah means "praise."

And you're not going to believe what God's Word says about Moab. In Psalm 108:9, God says, "Moab is my washbasin." In other words, God called Moab the dirty water that is left behind after someone has bathed. Moab was the disgusting, smelly, filthy leftover garbage. It was a place filled with pagan worship, including child sacrifice, idolatry, sin, and perversion of every kind. God had made it clear, time and again, that the Israelites were to stay away from that place.

So, this man took his wife and two sons, left the house of bread and praise, and went to a garbage can. Why would he do such a thing?

We don't know, really. But it sounds to me like he didn't trust God. He was like many of us, claiming a loose relationship with God; after all, he was a Hebrew. But when things got a little rough, he tucked tail and ran. In his blind, unspiritual state, he thought he'd be better off in a garbage heap than in the will of God.

Sound familiar? It should. It's a story that's been repeated over and over again throughout the history of God's people. We play at being Christians. We play at going to church. But we still live our lives pretty much the way we want. Then, when the heat is turned up, when we have to make the choice between walking in faith or jumping headfirst into the sin and garbage of this world, many of us will jump.

But there's good news. In Luke 15, Jesus shares the story of the lost son—the son who had it all and gave it up to go live in a pigsty. In the end, the son returned to his wealthy father, and the father welcomed him back with open arms.

That father is God, and that reckless son is every one of us. We are foolish to ever leave the shelter of God's arms, but we have a free will, and most of us, at one time or another, will exercise that free will and leave our Father.

The world, which promises great things, seems more attractive to us than a life of faith. But unlike God, the world seldom delivers on its promises, and we eventually realize that we've left God's riches for a garbage can. Still, we can always go home. And our Father, who loves us more than we will ever comprehend, will always welcome us back with open arms.

Cream and Sugar

How have I traded in God's best for something less?

Dear Father, I'm sorry to say I recognize myself in this foolish Hebrew family. Please forgive me for the times I've left the shelter of your perfect will, seeking to find something better in the world. Thank you for always forgiving me, always welcoming me home. Amen.

Second Cup

Moab is my washbasin, on Edom I toss my sandal; over Philistia I shout in triumph. (Psalm 108:9)

When he came to his senses, he said, "How many of my father's hired servants have food to spare, and here I am starving to death! I will set out and go back to my father and say to him: Father, I have sinned against heaven and against you." … But while he was still a long way off, the

father saw him and was filled with compassion for him; he ran to his son, threw his arms around him and kissed him. (Luke 15:17–18, 20)

THE LAST DROP

To disbelieve is easy; to scoff is simple;
to have faith is harder.

—Louis L'Amour

2

WHAT'S IN A NAME?

God's Word Says

The man's name was Elimelech, and his wife was Naomi. Their two sons were Mahlon and Kilion. They were Ephrathites from Bethlehem in the land of Judah. And when they reached Moab, they settled there. (Ruth 1:2 NLT)

First Cup

In ancient Hebrew society, names were of great significance. This is why the author includes them. Elimelech means, in Hebrew, "God is my King." Ironic, isn't it? A man whose very name reflected total trust and allegiance to his God, didn't trust God to provide for him and his family. He thought he could do a better job in a place that was known for its hostility and rebellion toward God. So he packed up his wife and sons, and they left God's country.

Naomi, it seems, was more aptly named. Her name means "pleasant, delightful, lovely." As we'll see in future verses, Naomi was indeed all these things. The names Mahlon and

Kilion mean, respectively, "sickly" and "puny." So maybe we should give Elimelech a break. His boys were sick, and there was famine in the land. Maybe he was just trying to take care of his family the best way he knew how.

Still, he should have known better. We all should know better than to seek refuge in the arms of a pagan, God-forsaken world, when our Father is always so gracious and good. We've all done it, though, so let's not be too hard on old Elimelech.

They were Ephrathites, which probably refers to their clan. Imagine that—they had a clan. They left parents, aunts, uncles, and cousins, who no doubt would have provided continued support, and went into a land where God was hated. And where God is hated, God's people are hated. It was true then, and it's true today.

Now, Elimelech didn't just make a quick trip to buy some groceries. He actually made his home in Moab. It doesn't matter whether or not he planned to ever return to Bethlehem. He belonged in Bethlehem—it was his home. Yet he chose to leave his home and make a new home in a place he had no business being. All because Mr. God-Is-My-King didn't really make God his King.

Oh, it's easy for us to point the finger at Elimelech, to question his faith, his motives, and his loyalty to God. But time and again in God's Word, we are warned against judging others. God didn't include this story in His Book so we could condemn Elimelech; He included it so we could learn from Him.

The world wants to paint a picture of God as harsh

and uncaring. But that's a lie. The world tries to beckon us, advertising itself as benevolent, glamorous, generous, exciting, loving … all lies. The world is the place we will suffer brutality and harsh blows, indifference, cruelty, and wickedness. But God, our loving, kind, benevolent Father, will always take care of us. And He will always welcome us home after the world has beaten us up. Elimelech was foolish to leave Bethlehem. Let's learn from his mistakes.

Cream and Sugar

How have I been deceived into thinking the world had something better to offer than God?

Dear Father, thank you for loving me even when I make foolish mistakes. Please help me not to make them. Amen.

Second Cup

The Lord is my shepherd, I shall not want. (Psalm 23:1 NKJV)

As a father has compassion on his children, so the Lord has compassion on those who fear him; for he knows how we are formed, he remembers that we are dust. (Psalm 103:13–14)

THE LAST DROP

When trouble comes,
focus on God's ability to care for you.

—Charles Stanley

3

LEGACY

God's Word Says

Now Elimelech, Naomi's husband, died, and she was left with her two sons. They married Moabite women, one named Orpah and the other Ruth. After they had lived there about ten years, both Mahlon and Kilion also died, and Naomi was left without her two sons and her husband. (Ruth 1:3–5)

First Cup

Oh, Elimelech. Look what he's done. He chose to leave God's country, chose to take his wife and two sickly sons into a pagan land, and now he's left them there stranded. I'm not blaming him for dying, although bad things always, always happen when we choose to journey outside the protection of God's borders. This just goes to show that what we do affects not only our own lives but also the lives of those we love.

Mahlon and Kilion may have been sickly, but apparently they had *something* going for them. They each managed to find a wife among the Moabite women (I guess they were lovers, not fighters). But Orpah and Ruth worshiped pagan gods. Mahlon and Kilion belonged to almighty God. And God, who is loving and benevolent and generous and kind, is also a jealous God. He loves us with a passionate, white-hot love. Just as a husband or wife has the right to expect his or her spouse not to commit adultery, God expects the same from His children.

That's how sin works, isn't it? We take one step, just as Elimelech did when he made the choice to leave God's Promised Land. Then the second step is easier, then the third, and so on. Then those around us, those who love us and look up to us, think, *Well, if so-and-so did it, it must not be that bad.* And before you know it, God's laws are being tossed aside left and right, and no one even pays attention to them anymore.

At first, our sin seems small, insignificant. Then it grows bigger and bigger. It snowballs and hurts everyone in its path, and often it's the innocent victims who take the brunt of the sting. Poor Naomi had her entire family wiped out. Perhaps they might have died anyway. Here she was, in a foreign land where God's people were despised. If Elimelech had never left Bethlehem, Naomi would have had the support of her clan. She would have had brothers, sisters, aunts, uncles, cousins, nieces, and nephews who would have taken her in, comforted her, and made sure she was cared for.

Now she was alone. She had to pay for her husband's disobedience to God all those years ago. This story breaks my heart, for it makes me think of all those I love, all those I will leave behind when I die. I don't want to leave them a bunch of messes they have to clean up. My actions affect them now and will continue to affect them after I'm gone.

There's a Steve Green song that prays for those who come after us to find we lived faithful lives. Elimelech made the choice not to be faithful. That choice hurt him, hurt his sons, and, most of all, hurt his beloved wife, who at that time in history probably had no say in the matter. What a sad, sad story. Our story doesn't have to be so sad. We always have the choice to be faithful or not. Obey God or not. Each small choice made in faith and obedience to God will build a legacy we can be proud to leave behind.

Cream and Sugar

Who are some of the people my choices will affect?

Dear Father, I want to make wise choices, both in the big and small things of life. Please help me to leave behind a legacy of faith for those I love. Amen.

Second Cup

But the mercy of the Lord is from everlasting to everlasting on those who fear Him, and His righteousness to his children's children, to such as keep His covenant, and to those who remember His commandments to do them. (Psalm 103:17–18 NKJV)

But if serving the Lord seems undesirable to you, then choose for yourselves this day whom you will serve, whether the gods your forefathers served beyond the River, or the gods of the Amorites, in whose land you are living. But as for me and my household, we will serve the Lord. (Joshua 24:15)

THE LAST DROP

We must begin thinking like a river
if we are to leave a legacy of beauty
and life for future generations.

—David Brower

4

GOING HOME

God's Word Says

Then Naomi got ready to return from the land of Moab with her daughters-in-law. She had heard in the land of Moab that the Lord had brought food to His people. So she left with her two daughters-in-law and went on the way toward the land of Judah. (Ruth 1:6–7 NLV)

First Cup

I am so impressed with Naomi. Here she was, a widow in a foreign land with a couple of widowed daughters-in-law. In a country where Jews were despised, during a time when women had few rights and there were no cars or airplanes, no telephones, no high-dollar comfort-sole shoes, she decided to go home. Walk home. Miles and miles and miles.

She had heard there was food back home. She knew there was family, love, and support back home. She could have stayed where she was and lived out her remaining days in regret, but she didn't. She found herself in a lousy situation, and she decided to do something about it.

Now, this journey was a dangerous one even for men. But three women? Traveling alone? Naomi had some pluck. Just as many animals in nature will journey their entire lives only to return home before they die, the true child of God will always, eventually, want to go home. Naomi had lived away from God and away from His promises long enough. She knew life was better within her Father's borders. So she started walking.

Oh, that every lost child of the King could know it's that simple! When we journey far from God, we can just turn around and start walking home. The journey may be a long one. It may be tiresome and uncomfortable, but we can know beyond any shred of doubt that we will be welcomed. Wanted. Celebrated. We can know with certainty that our Father has waited by the window for us. We can even know that He will meet us on the road and travel the journey with us.

It all begins with that first step. It's the most difficult one, for it's not taken with our feet but with our hearts. We must make the decision to go home. Once that decision is made, we can know that each small step we take will be met by two giant steps of our Father, who will run to meet us, wrap His arms around us, and welcome us home.

Cream and Sugar

How have I wandered away from God? What steps do I need to take to return to Him?

Dear Father, thank you for wanting me to come home. Amen.

Second Cup

Return, O Israel, to the Lord your God, for you have stumbled because of your iniquity. (Hosea 14:1 ESV)

For all have sinned and fall short of the glory of God, and all are justified freely by his grace through the redemption that came by Christ Jesus. (Romans 3:23–24)

THE LAST DROP

If men will not understand the meaning of judgment, they will never come to understand the meaning of grace.

—Dorothy Sayers

5

THE MOTHER-IN-LAW

God's Word Says

But Naomi said to her two daughters-in-law, "Go back each of you to your mother's house. May the Lord deal kindly with you, as you have dealt with the dead and with me. The Lord grant that you may find security, each of you in the house of your husband." Then she kissed them, and they wept aloud. (Ruth 1:8–9 NRSV)

First Cup

Naomi had no daughters by birth. When her sons married, they blessed her with the wives they chose. Though these women didn't share Naomi's faith in God, they were still women in a house full of men. They were faithful to her sons and delightful companions for her. I'm sure they laughed, cried, shopped, cooked, did laundry, and cleaned house together. In the unique way that only women understand, they bonded.

Unfortunately, Naomi knew what lay in store for her

daughters-in-law if they continued with her. Just as Naomi and her family had been despised in Moab, Ruth and Orpah would be despised in Bethlehem. After all, they were Moabites. And Jews didn't like Moabites. They had little hope of finding new husbands in Naomi's hometown.

It wasn't that Naomi wanted to leave her beloved girls behind. She had lost everything dear to her. To give up the last thread of connection to her sons, to say good-bye to these women who had been friends, confidantes, and daughters, must have broken her heart. But she loved them enough to lay aside her own wants and put them first. She wanted them to find happiness again, even if it meant sacrificing her own happiness.

That's where true happiness begins. When our lives are centered on ourselves, our capacity for peace, joy, and love is limited. But when we focus outward and spill our lives for those around us, our ability to love becomes boundless. And love, poured out freely to others, will come back to us many times over, providing more joy, fulfillment, and happiness than we ever could have found looking inward. Naomi was a wise woman.

Cream and Sugar

Have I been looking inward, focusing on my own desires, to find fulfillment? In what ways can I shift my focus outward?

Dear Father, please heighten my capacity to love. Amen.

Second Cup

So now I am giving you a new commandment: Love each other. Just as I have loved you, you should love each other. Your love for one another will prove to the world that you are my disciples. (John 13:34–35 NLT)

Don't just pretend to love others. Really love them. Hate what is wrong. Hold tightly to what is good. Love each other with genuine affection, and take delight in honoring each other. (Romans 12:9–10 NLT)

THE LAST DROP

Being deeply loved by someone
gives you strength, while loving someone
deeply gives you courage.

—Lao Tzu

6

THE SOLUTION

God's Word Says

Then she kissed them and they wept aloud and said to her, "We will go back with you to your people." But Naomi said, "Return home, my daughters. Why would you come with me? Am I going to have any more sons, who could become your husbands? Return home, my daughters; I am too old to have another husband. Even if I thought there was still hope for me—even if I had a husband tonight and then gave birth to sons—would you wait until they grew up? Would you remain unmarried for them? No, my daughters. It is more bitter for me than for you, because the Lord's hand has gone out against me!" (Ruth 1:9–13)

First Cup

Grab the Kleenex. This is at least a three-tissue moment. If this story were being played out on the silver screen, it would definitely be pegged as a chick flick. Oh, the drama, the drama!

Can't you just see these women, standing in the middle of the road, crying their eyes out? Naomi's heart is breaking because she knows that for their own good, she must send her girls back to their mothers. Orpah's and Ruth's hearts are breaking, for they've lost their husbands, and now their last flesh-and-blood connection to their lost loves is sending them away. Yet they know she's right. They need to go home. It's the only sensible thing to do.

During that time, if a woman was widowed, her dead husband's brother was to marry her and take care of her. Strange law, but it worked for them. But Naomi had no more sons. She had no husband and no prospects of any more children in her future. Even if she were to bear twin sons within a year, Orpah and Ruth would be old women by the time the twins were old enough to marry. There was no way around it. Ruth and Orpah needed to go home and find new husbands.

This situation only added to Naomi's bitterness. She had lost her husband and her sons. Now she was forced to give up her new daughters as well. She felt the Lord's hand had gone out against her, but she was wrong. God is love. He loves us beyond description. He is always for us and never against us.

Oh, He's against our sin. And He will discipline us, as a loving parent will discipline a child. But God didn't cause Naomi's pain. As a matter of fact, I'm sure God's heart was broken as He witnessed the suffering of His beloved daughter. She was angry, hurting, confused, and devastated; she wanted someone to blame. So she blamed the One who loved her more than anyone.

Have you ever felt that way, like God was against you? If so, think again. 1 John 3:1 says, "See what great love the Father has lavished on us, that we should be called children of God." 1 John 1:5 tells us, "God is light; in him there is no darkness at all." We live in a fallen, broken world where people get sick, hearts are broken, and life is just plain hard at times. God doesn't cause our problems. But He is the One who can heal our sickness, mend our broken hearts, and give us joy and peace and strength for our journeys. Instead of blaming God for our problems, we must remember that in all things He is our solution.

Cream and Sugar

How have I blamed God for my problems? How is He the solution?

Dear Father, please forgive me for blaming you when life gets difficult. Thank you for always being there to help me through the hard times. Amen.

Second Cup

I have told these things to you, so that in me you may have peace. In this world you will have trouble. But take heart! I have overcome the world. (John 16:33)

God is our refuge and strength, an ever-present help in trouble. (Psalm 46:1)

For no one is abandoned by the Lord forever. Though he brings grief, he also shows compassion because of the greatness of his unfailing love. For he does not enjoy hurting people or causing them sorrow. (Lamentations 3:31–33 NLT)

THE LAST DROP

If I were asked to give what I consider
the single most useful bit of advice for all
humanity it would be this: Expect trouble as an
inevitable part of life and when it comes, hold
your head high, look it squarely in
the eye and say, "I will be bigger than you.
You cannot defeat me."

—Ann Landers

7

THE DECISION

God's Word Says

And again they wept together, and Orpah kissed her mother-in-law good-bye. But Ruth clung tightly to Naomi. (Ruth 1:14 NLT)

First Cup

Here we are at the turning point. The crossroad. The place of decision. Naomi has urged her daughters-in-law to turn back. Orpah, brokenhearted, kissed her mother-in-law good-bye and turned around. Ruth, on the other hand, clung to Naomi. When she married, she became Naomi's daughter, and she refused to turn back.

Ruth, a Moabitess, had no way of knowing that one day, in the stable of an inn in Bethlehem, a baby would be born. She had no way of knowing that her great-great-great (many greats) grandson would be the promised Messiah. At that point, she didn't know if she would ever marry again or have children of her own. All she knew was she had to follow her mother-in-law. She felt compelled by a greater power to stay with Naomi.

Compelled, yes. Forced, no. God had plans for Ruth, for her offspring. Who knows, He may have had plans for Orpah too. We know that God invites all to come and join His family. But He never forces Himself on anyone. Ruth felt she needed to follow Naomi, and she did what she felt was right. Orpah, on the other hand, wept and kissed her mother-in-law good-bye. She didn't feel right about this decision, but she knew that in the long run, life would probably be easier for her in Moab than in Bethlehem. So she took the easy way.

Orpah did what many of us would have done. We reason things out in our minds. Sometimes, we make decisions based on what looks right on paper even when those decisions just don't feel right. Ruth stepped out in faith and followed her heart, and she was blessed because of it. If she had taken the easy way, she would have missed God's amazing favor on her life.

Now don't get me wrong. I'm not against reasoning things out. After all, God created us. He created our minds, and He created us with the ability to reason. We should absolutely use that God-given skill. But in the midst of our research, our facts, and our probabilities, we must never discount our gut feelings. Often, the feelings we get are from God Himself and His Holy Spirit. Once we have weighed all the facts and reasoned things out, we must be willing to step forward in faith and go against reason, if that is what we feel God is telling us to do.

Remember, God has given us His Word, and He will never tell us to do anything that goes against His laws. So, if we feel like robbing a bank, having an affair, or gossiping about a neighbor, we shouldn't act on those feelings. That would be sin. But if we seek God, pray, and weigh a decision based on God's Word and all the available facts, then we have done what we need to do to act responsibly. Sometimes the reasonable thing is the right thing. Other times, as in Ruth's case, the right thing is to go against reason and follow our heart. And we never know what God may have in store for those of us who are willing to step out in faith and follow Him. God worked through Ruth's faith to achieve an incredible result, as Matthew tells us: "Boaz the father of Obed, whose mother was Ruth, Obed the father of Jesse, and Jesse the father of King David … and Jacob the father of Joseph, the husband of Mary, and Mary was the mother of Jesus who is called the Messiah." (Matthew 1:5–6, 16)

Cream and Sugar

What decisions am I facing right now? Have I weighed them against God's Word? What do I feel God is leading me to do?

Dear Father, please help me trust you when I feel you're leading me to do something. Help me seek you in all things and make wise choices. Amen.

Second Cup

For what human being knows what is truly human except the human spirit that is within? So also no one comprehends what is truly God's except the Spirit of God. (1 Corinthians 2:11 NRSV)

But it is the spirit in a man and the breath of the All-powerful that gives him understanding. (Job 32:8 NLV)

THE LAST DROP

Every time I've done something that doesn't feel right, it's ended up not being right.

—Mario M. Cuomo

8

NO TURNING BACK

God's Word Says

Naomi said, "See, your sister-in-law has returned to her people and her gods. Return after your sister-in-law." (Ruth 1:15 NLV)

First Cup

Poor Ruth. She was trying her best to do what she thought was right. She clung to Naomi, clung to her decision to stay with her mother-in-law. And yet Naomi tried to persuade her to turn around.

That happens to us, as Christians, every single day. We wake up, determined to make the most of our new day. We decide that this day we will serve our Lord. We will make wise choices. We will walk with God and follow where He leads.

But it seems at every turn there are some well-meaning people, some circumstance, some obstacle trying to get us to go the other way. We want to do the right thing, but the right thing can be difficult—almost impossible. Each day, our faith is challenged. We will either stand firm in our decision to follow God, or we'll give in to the pressure and turn around.

God has given us many promises, but He never promised that walking in faith would be easy. As a matter of fact, in John 16:33, Jesus said, "In this world you will have trouble. But take heart! I have overcome the world." Standing strong in our faith is difficult in a world that doesn't respect faith. We'll be laughed at. We'll be looked down upon. We'll have all sorts of problems because of our belief in God. There's no doubt that, in some ways, a life lived without faith would be easier.

Don't be fooled! When we trade in our faith for an easier lifestyle, we trade one set of problems for an even bigger set. We also forfeit the wonderful, bountiful rewards that come to those who stand strong, who keep following God even though everyone tells them not to. Let's remember to stay focused, to keep our eyes on the prize. And whatever we do, we must never turn back.

Cream and Sugar

Who or what in my life influences me to move away from God? What can I do to lessen that influence?

Dear Father, help me to keep following you no matter what. Amen.

Second Cup

This day I call the heavens and the earth as witnesses against you that I have set before you life and death, blessings and curses. Now choose life, so that you and your children may live and that you may love the Lord your God, listen to his voice, and hold fast to him. For the Lord is your life, and he will give you many years in the land he swore to give to your fathers, Abraham, Isaac and Jacob. (Deuteronomy 30:19–20)

You did not choose Me, but I chose you and appointed you that you should go and bear fruit, and that your fruit should remain, that whatever you ask the Father in My name He may give you. (John 15:16 NKJV)

THE LAST DROP

The road to success is dotted with many tempting parking places.

—Author unknown

9

I PLEDGE ALLEGIANCE

God's Word Says

But Ruth said, "Do not urge me to leave you or turn back from following you; for where you go, I will go, and where you lodge, I will lodge. Your people shall be my people, and your God, my God. Where you die, I will die, and there I will be buried. Thus may the Lord do to me, and worse, if anything but death parts you and me." (Ruth 1:16–17 NASB)

First Cup

It doesn't take much to make me cry. But I don't like to cry in public! I'm not one of those pretty, dainty criers. My nose gets red and my face gets all splotchy. My mascara usually ends up all over my cheeks. Not exactly the image I like to present to the world.

Have you ever thought about the fact that Orpah shed just as many tears as Ruth? Orpah had an emotional experience and so did Ruth. The difference between these two women is that Ruth backed up her feelings with action. Orpah cried, but she returned to her former way of life.

I've been a dedicated church member for many decades now. During that time, I've witnessed a lot of emotional experiences. The test of whether or not one's decision to follow Christ is sincere isn't found in the number of tears shed; it's found in the evidence of a changed life.

Ruth's decision was steadfast. She had married into Naomi's family, a Jewish family, and she had taken her marriage vows seriously. She was no longer a Moabite but a Jew. She had pledged allegiance to the one true God and had experienced the freedom that came from that relationship. She had cast aside her idols, her pagan heritage, and her former way of life. She had no desire to return to it, for it had nothing to offer her.

She spoke to Naomi, but her pledge was to God. She would follow Naomi because Naomi would lead her to the Promised Land. She would stay with Naomi because Naomi symbolized her relationship with God. She had grown up in a pagan, hopeless culture, and now she had found hope in a God who loved her, who wanted the best for her, who had good things in store for her. She knew she was unworthy, but she wanted what Naomi had. She wanted it desperately.

She wanted God so desperately that she clung to the only person she knew who could lead her to Him. She left everything behind—every familiar person, place, and experience—and vowed to never look back. And she never did. Because of that steadfast decision to follow the one true God, she was blessed beyond measure.

Cream and Sugar

Have I had an emotional experience with God? Is there evidence in my life of a lasting transformation? If not, what do I need to change?

Dear Father, I want my actions to always reflect my decision to live for you. I love you. Amen.

Second Cup

But I lavish unfailing love for a thousand generations on those who love me and obey my commands. (Deuteronomy 5:10 NLT)

So, my dear brothers and sisters, be strong and immovable. Always work enthusiastically for the Lord, for you know that nothing you do for the Lord is ever useless. (1 Corinthians 15:58 NLT)

THE LAST DROP

Let's do more than say
"The Pledge of Allegiance." Let's live it!

—Emanuel Cleaver

10

IT GETS EASIER

God's Word Says

When Naomi saw that Ruth had firmly made up her mind to go with her, she stopped arguing with her. (Ruth 1:18 NCV)

First Cup

I love this little verse. Hidden within its words is the wisdom of the ages. Or at least the wisdom of the aged. Those of us who have lived a little, who have experienced some difficult things, have learned what Ruth learned: it gets easier.

Oh, I don't mean life gets easier, though it sometimes does. But rather, it gets easier to stand firm, the more we do it. In most every experience in life, pressure weakens us. It tears us down and wears us out. However faith in God never weakens us. It always makes us stronger.

As Ruth clung to Naomi, she clung to God. Her pledge to Naomi was a pledge to God. Unlike Orpah, who chose not to cling, Ruth held fast. And through the holding, her resolve was strengthened. She became more and more determined

44

to follow Naomi, to follow her God no matter what. And while Naomi's words caused Orpah to turn around, they did nothing for Ruth.

Finally, Naomi gave up and Ruth's journey became a little easier. As we live in faith, as we stand determined to follow our God, there will be people around us who will try to make us turn around. But if we cling to Him, God will give us strength, and God's strength will always outlast the strength of those who would discourage us. Hold on. They'll give up. And following God will get easier.

The longer we hold on, the stronger we'll become in our faith. The stronger we become, the smaller the obstacles around us will seem. Finally, one day we will discover that the very things that seemed to threaten our relationship to God will have disappeared. They're no longer a problem for us, for they now seem small and petty and weak in comparison to the strength we've gained through our faith in God.

Cream and Sugar

Who or what is making it difficult for me to have faith in God? What are some things I can do to stay strong in my faith, in spite of these obstacles?

Dear Father, thank you for giving me strength to endure through the pressures of life. Thank you for making me stronger so my problems seem smaller. And Father, just as you caused Naomi to leave Ruth alone, please make my current problem disappear. Amen.

Second Cup

Pray in the Spirit at all times and on every occasion. Stay alert and be persistent in your prayers for all believers every-where. (Ephesians 6:18 NLT)

THE LAST DROP

The difference between perseverance and obstinacy is that one comes from a strong will, and the other comes from a strong won't.

—Henry Ward Beecher

11

HOMECOMING

God's Word Says

So Naomi and Ruth went on until they came to the town of Bethlehem. When they entered Bethlehem, all the people became very excited. The women of the town said, "Is this really Naomi?" (Ruth 1:19 NCV)

First Cup

In the ten-year span from my late twenties to my late thirties, I had enough experiences to fill a lifetime. I moved three times and taught at that many schools. I gave birth to one child and adopted another. I survived infertility, a miscarriage, and a loved one's cancer. I went through numerous pets. I had many, many hairstyles and even lived a brief stint as a redhead. Ten years is a long time.

Naomi had left Bethlehem ten years earlier with a husband and two sons. She returned without them. She now had a daughter, a few more wrinkles, and probably some gray hair. Her life had changed drastically.

But now she was home. Her family recognized her, loved her, and celebrated her return.

That's how it is with family. That's especially how it is with God's family. Sometimes His children leave, though He never wants them to. Sometimes we choose to live for a long time away from Him, but He never stops loving us. He never stops wanting us to come home. And when we do return, with weathered souls and tired spirits, we create quite a stir in the heavenly realm.

I feel certain the angels hop around excitedly, calling our names and saying, "Look who's come home!" I know God recognizes us even from a distance, and waits eagerly for our arrival. I know He celebrates our return. He wraps His arms around us and says, "Can this be (your name), my long lost child?"

Naomi had changed. She had experienced great loss. We always experience loss when we choose to live away from God. But now she had returned. She still had a long way to go before the raw feeling inside went away; her journey of healing had just begun. Even so, she was at a place where she could heal.

She was safe.

She was loved.

She was home.

Cream and Sugar

Have I journeyed away from God? What steps do I need to take to go home?

Dear Father, thank you for always knowing me, even when I seem to have forgotten you. Thank you for always welcoming me home. Amen.

Second Cup

But if you return to me and obey my commands, I will gather your people from the far ends of the earth. And I will bring them from captivity to where I have chosen to be worshiped. (Nehemiah 1:9 NCV)

"Return to me, and I will return to you," says the Lord All-Powerful. (Malachi 3:7 NCV)

THE LAST DROP

God is at home;
it is we who have gone for a walk.

—Meister Eckhart

12

TEMPER TANTRUM

God's Word Says

But she replied to them, "Don't call me 'Naomi'! Call me 'Mara' because the Sovereign One has treated me very harshly. I left here full, but the Lord has caused me to return empty-handed. Why do you call me 'Naomi,' seeing that the Lord has opposed me, and the Sovereign One has caused me to suffer?" (Ruth 1:20–21 NET)

First Cup

Naomi, Naomi. What happened to the sweet, pleasant woman who left Bethlehem ten years earlier? Remember, her name means pleasant, but apparently, her sweet nature had its restrictions. She was pleasant as long as things went her way. She was even pleasant when things became a little difficult. Yet like most of us, she had a limit. And she was tired of being pleasant.

Here, we witness Naomi having a bit of a meltdown. "Don't call me Naomi!" she tells her long lost loved ones. "Don't call me pleasant. I'm tired of being pleasant! Call me Mara, which means bitter. I'm changing my name to reflect how I feel. God has not been good to me, and I'm angry at Him!"

Have you ever been angry with God? Have you believed He's brought misfortune on you? If so, you're not alone. Most of us have felt that way at one time or another. And do you know what? God can handle that. When we're weary, hurting, or even bitter, God already knows. He's aware of our deepest thoughts before we ever have them. Like the parent who holds the flailing, angry child, hushing them, lovingly calming the tantrum, God will hold us, even when we rant and accuse Him of not caring. He loves us that much. He will never let us go, even when we lash out at Him.

We must remember, however, that God is good. He is only good. He doesn't cause the bad things in this world. Sometimes, we bring bad things on ourselves. Other times, bad things happen simply because we live in a fallen, broken world. But He promised never to leave us, never to forsake us. Even in the midst of the worst circumstance, He is there, loving us, calming us, and comforting us.

Naomi claimed she went away full and came back empty. But isn't she forgetting someone? She went away without a daughter, and she came back with the most devoted, loyal, loving daughter anyone could ask for. Yes, she had lost much, but she wasn't empty. God hadn't deserted her. He sent her someone who would stay with her, so she wouldn't be alone. And just as He provided Naomi with something good, pure, and wonderful, He does the same for each of us.

When our circumstances are a mess, when we're at those melting points in our lives, we often forget to stop, take deep breaths, and recognize God's goodness. Our souls flail and kick and scream, and we have our temper tantrums at God, who must be responsible for the pain we feel. All the while, God holds us. All the while, He loves us. If we will calm down long enough to really look at our lives, we'll realize that His goodness has never ceased.

Cream and Sugar

Am I angry with God about something? (If so, tell Him about it now. He's ready to listen.)

Dear Father, thank you for holding onto me, even when I feel angry. Thank you for your constant goodness in my life. Amen.

Second Cup

You are bad and you know how to give good things to your children. How much more will your Father in heaven give good things to those who ask Him? (Matthew 7:11 NLV)

You have tasted that the Lord is good. (1 Peter 2:3)

THE LAST DROP

Forgiveness is the key that unlocks the door of resentment and the handcuffs of hate. It is a power that breaks the chains of bitterness and the shackles of selfishness.

—William Arthur Ward

13

HARVEST TIME

God's Word Says

So Naomi returned, and with her Ruth the Moabitess, her daughter-in-law, who returned from the land of Moab. And they came to Bethlehem at the beginning of barley harvest. (Ruth 1:22 NASB)

First Cup

When Naomi and her family had left Bethlehem ten years earlier, they were hoping to find life. Her husband had heard there was more food in Moab, so off they went, but instead of life, they found death. Again and again.

Now, as Naomi returns to Bethlehem, she returns to a full harvest. Life. Abundance. Renewal. Isn't that a perfect picture of our spiritual lives? Whenever we leave God, expecting to find something more, something better, we always end up destitute. But when we journey toward God, we journey toward new life, toward the abundant life that is only available to those who choose to live as His blessed children.

The other day, I read an interesting article about marketing and packaging. Satan is a master at glitzy, sparkly, glamorous packaging. He beckoned Naomi's family to Moab where there was supposedly plenty to eat. In Moab, they thought they'd find the exciting, exotic, abundant lifestyle they longed for. Glitzy packaging often hides a substandard product, and Satan's products are always lousy. Satan's wares may look good on the outside, but they bring heartache, disease, and death.

God, on the other hand, has no need to glitz up His product. The product itself really works! Faith in God always, always brings us to life, peace, and an abundance of spirit that needs no embellishment.

That's what God did for Naomi, and that is what He'll do for us. If the world's glamorous, empty packaging has fooled you, you're not alone. Satan has been in the business of drawing people away from God since the garden of Eden. If you find yourself living in regret and spiritual poverty, just come home! Come back to your Father. Come back to the harvest of peace, joy, and wisdom He has waiting for you as soon as you set foot back in His territory.

Cream and Sugar

How have I been fooled into believing the world's ways are better than God's ways?

Dear Father, thank you for the bountiful harvest that waits for me each time I come to you. Amen.

Second Cup

The Lord is compassionate and gracious, slow to anger, abounding in love. (Psalm 103:8)

If any of you lacks wisdom, you should ask God, who gives generously to all without finding fault, and it will be given to you. (James 1:5)

THE LAST DROP

The truth, of course, is that a billion falsehoods told a billion times by a billion people are still false.

—Travis Walton

14

WORKING GIRL

God's Word Says

Now Naomi had a relative on her husband's side, from the clan of Elimelek, a man of standing, whose name was Boaz. And Ruth the Moabitess said to Naomi, "Let me go to the fields and pick up the leftover grain behind anyone in whose eyes I find favor." Naomi said to her, "Go ahead, my daughter." So she went out and began to glean in the fields behind the harvesters. As it turned out, she found herself working in a field belonging to Boaz, who was from the clan of Elimelek. (Ruth 2:1–3)

First Cup

Did you know that God is so concerned about the poor that He made provisions for them? In Leviticus 23:22, He said, "When you reap the harvest of your land, do not reap to the very edges of your field or gather the gleanings of your harvest. Leave them for the poor and for the foreigner residing among you. I am the Lord your God." In this one law, God made sure the poor had food. He also made sure they worked for their food, since they had to go out and reap the corners. They had to glean or find what was left behind in the rest of the field as well. He knew that hard work is good for the soul and gives a person a sense of pride and accomplishment.

Ruth and Naomi, as widows, had no way of providing for themselves. Ruth knew this, and she didn't wait for someone to give them a handout. She knew where she could find food, so she decided to go get it.

I think Ruth probably puts many of us to shame. We've become so accustomed to our fast-food society that we don't like to wait for things, much less do back-breaking labor in order to get them. We want to pull into a drive-thru and have our orders ready by the time we count out our change. We've developed this mentality not only for food but for just about everything we need. We want what we want. We want it the easy way. And we want it now.

But have you noticed that, for all the stuff we have so easily at our fingertips, there's a real lack of satisfaction? When we don't work for something, we are robbed of the joy and fulfillment of knowing we earned it. God knew that within each of us there's an emptiness that far surpasses the hungry feeling in our bellies. He created us with a need to feel useful, needed, and proud of a job well done.

Is there something you want or need? Let's follow Ruth's example! Let's not sit around and wish, hope, and pray for it to drop into our laps. Instead, let's take some initiative, get off our comfy couches, and get to work. God will bless the person who works hard. While God always provides, His provision comes in the form of our ability to work hard. When we keep our shoulder to the wheel, He'll see we have what we need to keep our bodies and our spirits healthy.

Cream and Sugar

Do I have something I worked really hard for? Do I value it more than things I didn't work for?

Dear Father, please teach me to work hard for what I need. Amen.

Second Cup

Rich and poor have this in common: The Lord is the Maker of them all. (Proverbs 22:2)

If there is among you a poor man of your brethren, … you shall not harden your heart nor shut your hand from your poor brother, but you shall open your hand wide to him and willingly lend him sufficient for his need, whatever he needs. (Deuteronomy 15:7–8 NKJV)

THE LAST DROP

If this is going to be a Christian nation that doesn't help the poor, either we have to pretend that Jesus was just as selfish as we are, or we've got to acknowledge that He commanded us to love the poor and serve the needy without condition and then admit that we just don't want to do it.

—Stephen Colbert

15

WHO'S THAT GIRL?

God's Word Says

Just then Boaz arrived from Bethlehem and greeted the harvesters, 'The Lord be with you!' 'The Lord bless you!' they answered. Boaz asked the overseer of his harvesters, 'Who does that young woman belong to?' (Ruth 2:4–5 NIVUK)

First Cup

Boaz was one of the most eligible bachelors in Bethlehem. He was rich. He was powerful. And he was kind. Obviously, he had a good relationship with his workers, for he gave them a friendly greeting when he arrived at his field, and they responded with familiar respect. I can't help but wonder how many young Bethlehem girls had set their caps for this man.

But here, we witness a case of love at first sight. How romantic! Boaz saw Ruth, this little foreign widow, and he asked his foreman, "Who's that girl?" Or, in my own loose translation, he said, "Wow! What a babe! Where has she been all my life?"

Now, if you think it's just coincidence that of all the fields in Bethlehem, Ruth ended up in the field of the most eligible bachelor in town, you're mistaken. Ruth may not have had a clue, but God did. And God was setting the stage for a little romance.

My friends, we have no idea what wonderful things God has in store for us when we are faithful and follow him. Ruth had pledged her loyalty to God. She had sacrificed much to stay with Naomi. She had proven herself to be a self-starter and a hard worker. God was pleased with this little Moabitess. And He was getting ready to pour out some major blessings on her!

The beautiful thing is, Ruth didn't have a clue. She wasn't manipulating things, trying to find a husband. She was just going about her business, gathering barley, trying to provide for herself and her mother-in-law. I'm sure she was sweaty and tired, probably not looking her best. Her focus was on being faithful to her oath.

What an example to us all! So many times, we seek God's blessings instead of seeking God. When we take the focus off ourselves and just serve God, He will bless us and bless us, beyond what we could ever expect or imagine.

Cream and Sugar

Have I sought God's blessings—beauty, riches, popularity, etc.—instead of simply seeking God?

Dear Father, help me to focus on pleasing you, instead of on how you can bless me. Thank you for your goodness. Amen.

Second Cup

But just as it is written: "Things that no eye has seen, or ear heard, or mind imagined, are the things God has prepared for those who love him." (1 Corinthians 2:9 NET)

THE LAST DROP

If we never experience the chill of
a dark winter, it is very unlikely that we will ever
cherish the warmth of a bright summer's day.
Nothing stimulates our appetite for the simple
joys of life more than the starvation caused
by sadness or desperation. In order to
complete our amazing life journey successfully,
it is vital that we turn each and every
dark tear into a pearl of wisdom,
and find the blessing in every curse.

—Anthon St. Maarten

16

A GOOD NAME

God's Word Says

The servant answered, "She is the young Moabite woman who came back with Naomi from the country of Moab. She said, 'Please let me follow the workers cutting grain and gather what they leave behind.' She came and has remained here, from morning until just now. She has stopped only a few moments to rest in the shelter." (Ruth 2:6–7 NCV)

First Cup

Do you get the feeling this foreman may have been trying to discourage his master? "She's a Moabitess," he answered. Everyone knew Jews didn't like Moabites. "She's a beggar," he continued. But the more he talked about this woman, the more attractive she became. The truth of her character came shining through.

Proverbs 22:1 says, "A good name is more desirable than great riches; to be esteemed is better than silver or gold." Ruth had done nothing wrong; she had done everything right. She was loyal. She was faithful. She worked hard. And no matter what this foreman said about her, he couldn't disguise the beauty of her character.

Nothing in Scripture indicates that Ruth was accustomed to this type of labor. Yet she did what needed to be done, and she did it without complaint. Sometimes we view certain tasks as beneath us or unworthy of our skills. Sometimes, though, ya just gotta do what ya gotta do.

When faced with a difficult situation, our attitude will paint a detailed portrait of our character. We'll either face each task with quiet dignity and determined perseverance, or we'll complain, grumble, and procrastinate. And all the while, others will watch us and gather data. They'll draw their conclusions about what it means to be a child of God based on how we respond to whatever life throws at us.

Ruth was a beautiful woman, no doubt, but more importantly, she had a beautiful spirit. Ruth's character was discovered when she thought no one was watching. In the same way, our reputations are often determined not in the spotlight but in the shadows.

Cream and Sugar

What difficult things am I facing right now? How is my character holding up in response to those things?

Dear Father, please help me to live for you even when I think no one is watching. Please show me how to have a good name. Amen.

Second Cup

A good name is better than precious ointment. (Ecclesiastes 7:1 ESV)

My son, do not forget my teaching, but let your heart keep my commandments, for length of days and years of life and peace they will add to you. Let not steadfast love and faithfulness forsake you; bind them around your neck; write them on the tablet of your heart. So you will find favor and good success in the sight of God and man. (Proverbs 3:1–4 ESV)

THE LAST DROP

Love is the only mirror we
must use to judge ourselves
and others.

—Bodie Thoene

17

STAYING CLOSE

God's Word Says

Boaz went over to Ruth and said, "I think it would be best for you not to pick up grain in anyone else's field. Stay here with the women and follow along behind them, as they gather up what the men have cut. I have warned the men not to bother you, and whenever you are thirsty, you can drink from the water jars they have filled." (Ruth 2:8–9 CEV)

First Cup

There's no doubt about it—Boaz was smitten. He had no reason to want a poor widow woman coming into his fields. There's no indication that anyone else was there gleaning. But Boaz instructed Ruth to glean only in his field. Not only that, but he spread his cloak of protection around her. He told her, "You come back here as often as you wish, and don't go anywhere else. Stay with the women, drink when you're thirsty, and my men will leave you alone. You're safe here."

In those days, a woman alone was open to all kinds of

ridicule, insults, and even physical harm. Ruth could have had a hard road ahead. Boaz, however, made it clear that as long as she stayed near him, he would protect her and see that her needs were met.

The same is true for each of us. Our Father promises to meet our needs and to provide a measure of protection, as long as we don't go wandering off. As long as we stay close to Him, stay within His shadow, then our lives are easier. Our Daddy will take care us.

But when we choose, like Naomi's husband did, to wander away from our Father's protection, we will experience more hard knocks than we need to. This world won't treat us with the same gentle, loving care and protection our Father offers. In this world, we will be insulted, kicked around, taken advantage of, and even physically harmed. When we wander away from our Father, and the bullies of this world come, we're on our own. And usually, we don't do so well on our own.

Just as Boaz wanted Ruth to stay close, our loving Father longs for us to stay near Him. When we do, we reap the benefits of His promises. When we obey Him and seek His presence daily, we can know that He'll provide for us, protect us, and shower us with His love.

Cream and Sugar

Have I suffered consequences I didn't have to suffer because of my choice to wander away from God?

Dear Father, thank you for your promises. Please help me to stay close to you. Amen.

Second Cup

Come near to God and he will come near to you. (James 4:8)

The Lord is near to all who call on him, to all who call on him in truth. (Psalms 145:18)

THE LAST DROP

How far is heaven? It's not very far.
When you live close to God,
it's right where you are.

—Author unknown

18

FINDING FAVOR

God's Word Says

Then she fell on her face, bowing to the ground and said to him, "Why have I found favor in your sight that you should take notice of me, since I am a foreigner?" (Ruth 2:10 NASB)

First Cup

When Ruth followed Naomi to Bethlehem, she knew what she was in for. She had been fairly warned. She was a foreigner—and the worst kind of foreigner, a Moabitess. She was a poor widow woman in a strange land. She expected nothing but hatred and disdain. But here, in the eyes of a rich and powerful man, she found favor!

Perhaps Ruth didn't have access to a mirror, or she would have obviously seen what Boaz saw. She was a beautiful woman. Not only that, her reputation had preceded her, and she was known to be kind, loyal, and hardworking. She was attractive in body and in spirit. That's why Boaz fell in love with her.

We, on the other hand, have nothing. When God looks

at us, He doesn't care about physical beauty. He cares only about our hearts, and we are sinful to the core. We are born into sin—it's our nature. And God hates sin; He can't stand to even look at it.

So, although Ruth perhaps had lovely qualities that would attract Boaz, we have nothing within ourselves to attract God. It is we, not Ruth, who should fall on our faces before our God. We should exclaim, "Why have I found such favor in your eyes that you notice me, a sinner?"

The answer to that question isn't found with us but with God. He doesn't love us because we deserve to be loved. He loves us because it is His nature to love. He is love. And He loves us with a passion, with fervor and zeal that caused Him to give the ultimate gift for us—His own Son. We have found favor with Him simply because He loves us, He loves us, He loves us! And nothing can ever separate us from that love.

Cream and Sugar

Doesn't it feel good to know I don't have to be good enough, smart enough, or pretty enough to earn God's love? He loves me at my worst, and He'll never, ever take His love away from me.

Dear Father, I fall on my face before you, knowing you have no reason to love me. Thank you, thank you, thank you for loving me anyway! Amen.

Second Cup

For I am convinced that neither death nor life, neither angels nor demons, neither the present nor the future, nor any powers, neither height, nor depth, nor anything else in all creation will be able to separate us from the love of God that is in Christ Jesus our Lord. (Romans 8:38–39)

For I, the Lord your God, hold your right hand; it is I who say to you, "Fear not, I am the one who helps you." (Isaiah 41:13 ESV)

In this is love, not that we have loved God but that he loved us and sent his Son to be the propitiation for our sins. (1 John 4:10 ESV)

But God shows his love for us in that while we were still sinners, Christ died for us. (Romans 5:8 ESV)

THE LAST DROP

Though we are incomplete, God loves us completely. Though we are imperfect, He loves us perfectly. Though we may feel lost and without compass, God's love encompasses us completely. ... He loves every one of us, even those who are flawed, rejected, awkward, sorrowful, or broken.

—Dieter F. Uchtdorf

19

BLESSABLE

God's Word Says

Boaz replied, "I've been told all about what you have done for your mother-in-law since the death of your husband—how you left your father and mother and your homeland and came to live with a people you did not know before. May the Lord repay you for what you have done. May you be richly rewarded by the Lord, the God of Israel, under whose wings you have come to take refuge." (Ruth 2:11–12)

First Cup

Do you want God's blessings? It's a silly question, really. Of course you do, and so do I. We all want to live in God's favor, to experience His good gifts, and to be rewarded for our good deeds. And we can certainly have all of that, but there's a catch.

If we want to be blessed, we have to be blessable.

Casts a new light on the whole blessings idea, doesn't it? Now, don't get me wrong. God is so good and so loving that He pours out blessings on everyone. Everyone. We all have air to breathe, sunshine, and moonlight. We all get to experience the laughter of children—just take a walk in the park! We all are blessed. But God does have a way of sending extra-special concentrations of blessings to those with whom He's pleased.

All too often, we want to live our lives exactly as we choose, without a thought to what would please our heavenly Father. Oh, we may go to church now and then. We may even cast a few pennies or dollars in the collection plate from time to time. Or, to appease our misplaced guilt, we may make a single grand gesture, such as giving half our Christmas bonus to an orphanage in a Third World country. These are all good things, but they don't exactly make us blessable. They don't put us in right standing with God.

What God wants from us more than anything is consistency. He wants to see that, over the long haul, we are committed to Him. He wants us to make the little choices, day after day after day, to live for Him. He wants to see that we will serve Him in good times, in bad times, in mediocre times. He wants us to be reliable in our character and in our faith.

Ruth had consistency. She made the choice to forsake her idols, to leave her family, and to serve God. She made the decision to stand by her mother-in-law, and she didn't waver from that decision. Each of her actions, big or small, gave testimony to her commitment, her love, and her dedication to Naomi and to God.

72

Boaz saw the same thing everyone else saw—the same thing God saw. Boaz asked God to bless this woman, and God did. And He will do the same for each person who consistently lives for Him. He will bless and bless those who make themselves blessable.

Cream and Sugar

Am I blessable?

Dear Father, please help me to show consistency in my choices as I try to live for you. Amen.

Second Cup

But blessed is the one who trusts in the Lord, whose confidence is in him. They will be like a tree planted by the water that sends out its roots by the stream. It does not fear when heat comes; its leaves are always green. It has no worries in a year of drought and never fails to bear fruit. (Jeremiah 17:7–8)

Commit to the Lord whatever you do, and he will establish your plans. (Proverbs 16:3)

Worship the Lord your God, and his blessing will be on your food and water. (Exodus 23:25)

THE LAST DROP

God doesn't bless us just to make us happy;
He blesses us to make us a blessing.

—Warren W. Wiersbe

20

HUMBLE

God's Word Says

Then she said, "I have found favor in your sight, my lord, for you have comforted me and indeed have spoken kindly to your maidservant, though I am not like one of your maidservants." (Ruth 2:13 NASB)

First Cup

Ruth was beautiful. She was kind, loyal, and hardworking. But do you know what her most attractive quality was? Her humility. She gave freely of herself and expected nothing in return.

I wish I could be like Ruth. I believe there's a little Pharisee in each of us, wanting to rise up and be noticed for our good deeds. We want to be thought of as important, as special, as intelligent, beautiful, and worthy. Ruth, however, was truly surprised when this important man showed her a little consideration. She didn't expect attention or kindness, which made Boaz want to show her even more attention and kindness.

Maybe we can blame our me-centered culture. Perhaps

we can blame our old sin nature. Whatever the reason, few of us are truly humble. We give, expecting. We work hard, wanting to be noticed and wanting to be promoted. We are kind, but only as long as we are shown kindness. We don't want others to look down on us. We try to hide the fact that we look down on others.

God has called us to a lifestyle that is both radical and uncomfortable at times. He wants us to—get this—treat others like they're better than us. He wants us to "do nothing of selfish ambition or conceit, but with humility consider others more important than yourselves" (Philippians 2:3 TLV). Can you believe that? This kind of humility is so foreign to our way of thinking that it's almost like reading another language. Yet the rewards of this type of lifestyle are great.

Ruth's attitude sealed the deal for Boaz. He was taken with this humble little Moabitess who treated him and others with such deference, and because of this, he would eventually marry her and put her in a place of great honor. In the same way, our Lord and Master is quite pleased when He sees one of His children treating His other children with respect and honor, putting themselves in the shadows so others can shine. God is pleased with humility.

Cream and Sugar

What adjustments do I need to make to my attitude toward others?

Dear Father, please teach me to put others before myself. I want to be humble. Amen.

Second Cup

Whoever exalts himself will be humbled, and whoever humbles himself will be exalted. (Matthew 23:12 ESV)

Do nothing from rivalry or conceit, but in humility count others more significant than yourselves. Let each of you look not only to his own interests, but also to the interests of others. Have this mind among yourselves, which is yours in Christ Jesus, who, though he was in the form of God, did not count equality with God a thing to be grasped, but emptied himself, by taking the form of a servant, being born in the likeness of men. (Philippians 2:3–11 ESV)

Humble yourselves, therefore, under the mighty hand of God so that at the proper time he may exalt you. (1 Peter 5:6 ESV)

THE LAST DROP

There is nothing noble in being superior to your fellow man; true nobility is being superior to your former self.

—Ernest Hemingway

21

FAIRY TALE

God's Word Says

At mealtime Boaz said to her, "Come over here. Have some bread and dip it in some wine vinegar." When she sat down with the harvesters, he offered her some roasted grain. She ate all she wanted and had some left over. (Ruth 2:14)

First Cup

My, my. I just love a good romance story, don't you? Boaz has just met this woman, and he's already asking her on a lunch date. He's rich, he's powerful, and he's going after this poor little widow woman. It's an early version of Cinderella! I almost wonder if there were harps playing in the background.

If you haven't guessed by now, I'm one of those hopeless romantics who becomes weepy-eyed watching the Hallmark channel. I get butterflies in my stomach when I see love blossoming. So really, those butterflies ought to soar all the time because I have a Handsome Prince—no, a King! And He loves me with all His heart.

He loves me so much, He invites me to spend time with Him. As a matter of fact, He never leaves me alone. He loves me so much, He gives me unexpected gifts. He sees that my needs are met. He protects me. And when He chooses to bless me, He always gives more than I ever expect or need. My cup runneth over.

Ruth attracted the attention of the wealthy landowner. For reasons that are beyond comprehension, we attract the attention of our King. He beckons us to eat with Him, walk with Him, and talk with Him. Just as Boaz gave Ruth more than she needed, God blesses us with abundant blessings. He loves us. He wants us. And He relentlessly pursues us.

Boaz wanted Ruth's heart. God wants our heart. It's the stuff fairy tales are made of, but this is no fairy tale. The love God has for us is the real deal. Now, if that doesn't make your heart sing, I don't know what will.

Cream and Sugar

How has God shown His love to me? How has He pursued my heart?

Dear Father, thank you for loving me, for pursuing me and seeing something in me that is worth your attention. Please help me to be worthy of that kind of love by giving you my whole heart. Amen.

Second Cup

Your love, O Lord, reaches to the heavens, your faithfulness to the skies. Your righteousness is like the mighty mountains, your justice like the great deep. O Lord, you preserve both man and beast. How priceless is your unfailing love! Both high and low among men find refuge in the shadow of your wings. (Psalm 36:5–7)

THE LAST DROP

Fairy tales do not tell children the dragons exist. Children already know that dragons exist. Fairy tales tell children the dragons can be killed.

—G. K. Chesterton

22

WHAT IF?

God's Word Says

As she got up to glean, Boaz gave orders to his men, "Even if she gathers among the sheaves, don't embarrass her. Rather, pull out some stalks for her from the bundles and leave them for her to pick up, and don't rebuke her." (Ruth 2:15–16)

First Cup

Boaz was a genuinely good man. Jewish law required that he let Ruth, or anyone else for that matter, gather from the corners of the field. He also had to let her have what was left behind after the crop had been harvested. But Boaz went above and beyond the minimum requirements and made sure Ruth had plenty. He also did it in a way that would not embarrass her.

It's tempting, sometimes, to do the minimum and nothing more. We tithe, but we don't give more than 10 percent. We give our cast-off clothes to the poor, but we only purchase new things for ourselves. We give just enough to meet the least possible requirements by whatever standards we choose to live by. And we pat ourselves on the back and go on our merry way.

What if we decided to give more than the minimum? What if, instead of simply donating our too-tight, faded, stained clothing, we slipped a few brand-new designer clothes with the tags still on into the donation bag? What if we gave 12 percent instead of 10? What if, instead of a few pennies and dimes, we handed the guy on the corner a steaming-hot Big Mac and fries, with a large soda? And what if we decided to give more than the minimum *every* time?

What if, instead of showing up a few minutes late for work and leaving a few minutes early, we did the opposite? What if, instead of just inviting that person to church, we offered to pick them up and then take them to lunch afterward? Just think of the difference we could make in this world if we made it a lifestyle—a habit of always giving more than is expected.

Yes, Boaz was a genuinely good man. And this world is starving for genuinely good, godly people to make a difference, to give more, to love more, to go the extra mile. You can be that person, and so can I, if we just raise the bar a little. Let's imitate Boaz. Even more, let us be imitators of God, who gave much, much more than the minimum. He gave everything He had because of love.

Cream and Sugar

What are some practical ways I can give a little more than is expected of me?

Dear Father, thank you for giving so much for me. Please help me not to be stingy with your blessings. Help me to give generously of myself, so others may see your love. Amen.

Second Cup

Jesus Christ laid down his life for us. And we ought to lay down our lives for our brothers. (1 John 3:16)

You have heard that it was said, "An eye for an eye and a tooth for a tooth." But I say to you, Do not resist the one who is evil. But if anyone slaps you on the right cheek, turn to him the other also. And if anyone would sue you and take your tunic, let him have your cloak as well. And if anyone forces you to go one mile, go with him two miles. Give to the one who begs from you, and do not refuse the one who would borrow from you. (Matthew 5:38–42 ESV)

Whatever one sows, that will he also reap. For the one who sows to his own flesh will from the flesh reap corruption, but the one who sows to the Spirit will from the Spirit reap eternal life. And let us not grow weary of doing good, for in due season we will reap, if we do not give up. (Galatians 6:7–9 ESV)

THE LAST DROP

Let no one ever come to you without leaving better and happier.

—Mother Teresa

23

SPILLING OVER

God's Word Says

So Ruth picked up grain in the field until evening. Then she separated the barley from the straw. The barley weighed 30 pounds. She carried it back to town. Her mother-in-law saw how much she had gathered. Ruth also brought out the food left over from the lunch Boaz had given her. She gave it to Naomi. (Ruth 2:17–18 NIRV)

First Cup

When I was a little girl, my grandmother and my aunt were the cooks for the Stephen F. Austin State University Forestry Department. These young forestry students spent all day tromping through the woods, and they'd return to the "camp" with massive appetites. Memaw and Aunt Doris always had delicious-smelling, heavenly-tasting food waiting for them. And when I visited, guess what? I ate juicy fried chicken, homemade yeast rolls, and steaming peach cobbler till my heart (and stomach) was content. I had done

83

nothing to deserve such a treat; I just reaped the benefits of being in their family. I got to share in the abundant blessings those two ladies provided.

In the same way, Naomi received some residual benefits because her daughter-in-law had worked hard. Naomi was blessed because Ruth was beautiful, humble, and kind. In a way, Ruth had earned her blessing. She had kept her pledge to God, and God was pleased. He rewarded Ruth, and Naomi reaped the benefits.

It's important for us to understand that our actions really do affect other people. Naomi's husband chose to leave God's Promised Land, and Naomi suffered because of it. Ruth chose to be faithful to God and to her mother-in-law, and Naomi was blessed.

How many times have we hurt those we love the most, simply because we've made sinful, rebellious choices? We're foolish to think our actions don't affect the people around us. When we make good choices, when we choose to obey God, we please Him. And when He is pleased, He pours out blessings. Those blessings then spill over to the people we love.

Most of us look for ways to show our loved ones how much we care about them. We see to their needs. We buy them things. We write poetry, prepare special meals, and do their laundry. But the best thing we can do for the people we love is to live lives that please God. In so doing, we will cause His rich, abundant blessings to spill over from our lives into theirs. And that's even better than Memaw's fried chicken.

Cream and Sugar

How have I been included in someone else's blessings?

Dear Father, thank you for showing me more and more reasons to live for you. I love you. Amen.

Second Cup

But the Lord's love for those who have respect for him lasts forever and ever. Their children's children will know that he always does what is right. (Psalm 103:17 NIRV)

He shows mercy to those who have respect for him, from parent to child down through the years. (Luke 1:50 NIRV)

THE LAST DROP

"It is our choices, Harry, that show what we
truly are, far more than our abilities."

—J. K. Rowling, *Harry Potter and the Chamber of Secrets*

24

WHO DID THIS?

God's Word Says

Her mother-in-law said to her, "Where did you glean today, and where did you work? May he who took notice of you be blessed." So she told her mother-in-law with whom she had worked, and said, "The name of the man with whom I worked today is Boaz." (Ruth 2:19–20 MEV)

First Cup

Have you ever carried twenty-two liters of groceries into your home? I have, and it takes several trips. Ruth brought home an ephah of barley, which is about twenty-two liters. It would have fed Ruth and Naomi for more than a week.

Naomi took one look at all the bags of groceries, and she didn't congratulate Ruth. She didn't say, "Well done, daughter. I can see you've worked hard." The amount of barley Ruth brought home went well beyond what any normal woman could gather in a day. Naomi knew that someone had taken notice of Ruth.

God works that way sometimes. He likes to get the glory,

so He does things in our lives that clearly have nothing to do with our abilities. He allows us to get into situations where we feel limited, circumstances that are beyond our talents, beyond our control. And then He works miracles. He does such great things that others have no choice but to say, "Who took notice of you?"

It's good for us to work hard and use our abilities for God. Sometimes, however, we resist doing things for Him because we don't think we have the ability to do what He asked. But that's exactly what He wants from us! Then He can get all the glory for what is done.

Ruth could have said, "Why bother to work all day? I won't gather that much anyway. It's hot and I'm tired. I have enough for lunch. I'll just go home." But she didn't. She stayed and she worked hard, even though she knew her ability was limited. And lo and behold, God sent Boaz to the fields that day. Ruth was blessed through Boaz, and God got the glory.

Cream and Sugar

Is God leading me to do something I don't feel qualified to do?

Dear Father, I want you to get the credit for every good thing in my life. Thank you for giving me opportunities to work hard and stretch my abilities, so you can get the glory. Amen.

Second Cup

Whatever you do, do your work heartily, as for the Lord rather than for men, knowing that from the Lord you will receive the reward of the inheritance. It is the Lord Christ whom you serve. (Colossians 3:23–24 NASB)

For the Son of Man is going to come with his angels in the glory of his Father, and then he will repay each person according to what they have done. (Matthew 16:27)

THE LAST DROP

Work diligently. Work hard. Focus.
Perform as if you are at the Olympics.
One day, unexpectedly, it will start paying off.

—Joan F. Marques

25

RESCUED

God's Word Says

So Naomi said to her daughter-in-law, "May he be blessed by
Adonai who has not stopped his kindness to the living or to
the dead." Then Naomi said to her, "This man is closely related
to us, one of our kinsmen-redeemers." (Ruth 2:20 TLV)

First Cup

The kinsman-redeemer law is a unique and beautiful law
that paints a wonderful picture of our relationship to Christ.
In Jewish culture, all property was divided up and given to
families or clans. The property was intended to stay in the
family. If a person was unable to pay his bills or tend his
land, he could sell the land or could sell himself into slavery.
But every fifty years came the Year of Jubilee, when every
mortgage was canceled and every Jewish slave set free. So at
the Year of Jubilee, all land was returned to its original owner
and every slave was free to return to his family.

If, during those fifty years, a close relative wanted to buy

89

back the land or buy out the slave's contract, he could. So if a rich uncle decided he wanted to restore his nephew's land to him, or if a wealthy cousin decided he wanted to buy out his cousin's contract and set him free, then that close relative had the right to do so. He also needed to be willing and able to take responsibility for any and all debt.

Basically, a kinsman-redeemer was a close relative who came to the rescue of someone who could not rescue himself. Jesus is our Kinsman-Redeemer! God is our Father, and Jesus is our brother. As our close relative, Jesus has the right to come to our rescue. He alone has the ability to pay the debt we owe for our sin, for He is the spotless lamb. And He stepped up to the plate and was willing to pay that price for us with His life.

Let's face it. We were in a hopeless situation. We are all sinners, and God doesn't allow sinners to enter His presence. We had to pay the debt for our sin and be cleared. But we couldn't do that, could we? For the wages of sin is death; the only way we could pay for our sin was to die!

Sounds pretty hopeless, but Jesus, our Kinsman-Redeemer, rode up on His white horse and saved us. He said, "I'll do it. I'll die for (your name)." And He did.

Then the most amazing thing happened. He conquered death itself and rose again. Now, if you or I had died for our own sins, we would not have conquered death. We would have experienced eternal death, but because of Jesus, we have eternal life. He redeemed us, my friend, and He holds out a redemption receipt to each of us as a gift. All we have to do is take it.

Have you accepted that gift? If so, praise God! If not, what's holding you back?

Cream and Sugar

If you wish to accept Jesus' gift, all you have to do is tell Him. You can use the prayer below as a guide:

Dear Jesus, thank you for paying the price I couldn't pay for my sin. I accept your gift to me, and I want to live the rest of my life as a thank-you to you. Amen.

Second Cup

All my bones will say: "Adonai, who is like You, rescuing the poor from one too strong for him, the poor and needy from one who robs him?" (Psalm 35:10 TLV)

THE LAST DROP

The priceless gift of life is love, with the help from God above. Love can change the human race, make this world a better place.

—Natalia Love

26

DREAMBOAT

God's Word Says

Then Ruth the Moabitess said, "He even said to me, 'Stay close to my workers until they have finished the entire harvest.'" Naomi answered her daughter-in-law Ruth, "It is good, my daughter-in-law, that you go out with his female workers, so that you will not be harmed in another field." So she stayed close to Boaz's female workers, gleaning until both the barley harvest and the wheat harvest were completed. Meanwhile she lived with her mother-in-law. (Ruth 2:21–23 TLV)

First Cup

Boaz … (heavy sigh). What a dreamboat! He was single. He was kind, thoughtful, and generous. He was wealthy. And he was in love with Ruth. For about six weeks, Ruth went to Boaz's field to glean. She was protected and well fed. In those fields, she found love.

When Ruth arrived in Bethlehem, she expected to always

be an outcast. She didn't care about that though. Her heart had been broken. Her husband had died, and if she couldn't have him, she would at least stay with his mother. She would live with her mother-in-law for the rest of her days, in a land where she expected to be a servant and an outcast.

Yet, since God is good, and He doesn't want us to live with perpetual broken hearts. Oh, we all have seasons of sadness, but with God, joy comes in the morning! We may experience the darkest of nights, the saddest of trials, and the harshest of circumstances. But where God is, there is hope. Where God is, there are good things in store. God loves His children, and He loves to reward those who love Him in return.

I can look back at my own life. I have experienced some pretty rotten things; we all have. But God heals. When we follow Him, He will take us from a barren land to a land filled with milk and honey—or with barley and dreamboats, as in Ruth's case.

Is your heart broken? Like Ruth, have you experienced a deep and tragic loss? Has someone betrayed you? Do you feel there's no hope for happiness in your future? If so, you're mistaken. God loves you, and if you'll just keep following Him, He will lead you out of the desert. He will heal your heart and replace what you've lost with something wonderful.

Cream and Sugar

Has my heart been broken? Can I trust God to bring me through this broken time into something beautiful?

Dear Father, thank you for healing and for hope. Amen.

Second Cup

The Lord is close to the brokenhearted; he rescues those whose spirits are crushed. (Psalms 34:18 NLT)

THE LAST DROP

Heaven doesn't ignore cries
of a broken heart.

—Toba Beta

MATCHMAKER, MATCHMAKER (PART 1)

God's Word Says

Naomi her mother-in-law said to her, "My daughter, I need to seek some security for you, so that it may be well with you. Now here is our kinsman Boaz, with whose young women you have been working. See, he is winnowing barley tonight at the threshing floor. Now wash and anoint yourself, and put on your best clothes and go down to the threshing floor; but do not make yourself known to the man until he has finished eating and drinking. When he lies down, observe the place where he lies; then, go and uncover his feet and lie down; and he will tell you what to do." She said to her, "All that you tell me I will do." So she went down to the threshing floor and did just as her mother-in-law had instructed her. (Ruth 3:1–6 NRSV)

First Cup

In Jewish law, a childless, widowed woman had the right to claim one of her deceased husband's brothers as her husband. This protected the land, which would be inherited by her future children. More importantly, it protected the woman from becoming destitute. If, as in Ruth's case, there were no brothers, she could claim the closest relative to her husband. She had that right, and she could even take the man to court if he refused to marry her. If he still refused, he would be publicly disgraced.

The ball was in Ruth's court, but she didn't know that. She wasn't familiar with Jewish law. Boaz had shown his interest in her, but he really had no right to ask her to marry him. She had to somehow make the move. She had to claim him as her kinsman-redeemer.

Naomi decided that enough was enough. It was clear these two young people were crazy about each other, but this relationship was going nowhere fast. Ruth didn't have a clue how to tell Boaz she was interested, so Naomi took charge. She said, "Get dressed in your prettiest dress, and put on some perfume." (Up to this point, Boaz had only seen Ruth in her work clothes, all hot and sweaty.)

Now, it seems strange that Naomi told her to go sleep at Boaz's feet, but one thing is certain. Naomi wanted to leave no room for guessing. She wanted Boaz to know, without a doubt, that Ruth was interested. Who knows? Maybe Ruth was shy. Maybe Naomi knew this was the only way to get the message across. It was common for a servant to lie at the feet of the master and even share the covers. By doing this, Ruth was saying, "I'm yours if you want me."

Much like Boaz, God has done everything to show His interest in us. He has given us air to breathe and water to drink. He has sent snow in winter and bouquets of flowers in spring. Then, in the greatest act of love of all time, He sent His Son to die for us. Now the ball is in our court. He won't force Himself on us. Like Ruth, we must choose to go to our Master and say, "I'm yours."

Cream and Sugar

In what ways has God shown His interest in me today?

Dear Father, I am the servant. You are the master. I'm yours. Amen.

Second Cup

Indeed, rarely will anyone die for a righteous person—though perhaps for a good person someone might actually dare to die. But God proves his love for us in that while we still were sinners Christ died for us. Much more surely then, now that we have been justified by his blood, will we be saved through him from the wrath of God. (Romans 5:7–9 NRSV)

THE LAST DROP

God loves us the way we are, but he loves us too much to leave us that way.

—Leighton Ford

28

MATCHMAKER, MATCHMAKER (PART 2)

God's Word Says

Naomi her mother-in-law said to her, "My daughter, I need to seek some security for you, so that it may be well with you. Now here is our kinsman Boaz, with whose young women you have been working. See, he is winnowing barley tonight at the threshing floor. Now wash and anoint yourself, and put on your best clothes and go down to the threshing floor; but do not make yourself known to the man until he has finished eating and drinking. When he lies down, observe the place where he lies; then, go and uncover his feet and lie down; and he will tell you what to do." She said to her, "All that you tell me I will do." So she went down to the threshing floor and did just as her mother-in-law had instructed her. (Ruth 3:1–6 NRSV)

First Cup

Jewish laws and customs are unique and beautiful. Ruth, coming from a pagan background, had little hope of ever understanding Jewish ways. She had little hope of ever getting it right, without some help. Praise God! Naomi, who was Jewish by birth, was cheering for Ruth. She wanted Ruth to understand the Hebrew culture. She wanted to see her daughter-in-law find a husband who would love and care for her. So she helped Ruth.

In this touching love story, Naomi paints a picture of the Holy Spirit. God's ways are not our ways. They really make no sense to the common man. We have no hope of ever understanding the mind of God, of ever becoming like God, without a little help. But we do have help! We have the Holy Spirit, who makes Himself available to all who invite him. And with His guidance, the things of God become clear.

There's no getting around it. God's ways can be difficult to grasp sometimes. We don't understand holy God because His ways are foreign to us. We are unholy and sinful by nature. If we want to become like God, we need some help. Just as Naomi helped Ruth, the Holy Spirit will help us. God's Holy Spirit is cheering for us! He wants us to have a right relationship with God, and if we let Him, He will show us how. Like Ruth, we must be willing to do what the Holy Spirit tells us.

Ruth could have said, "That's ridiculous! You want me to do what? That makes no sense at all." She could have scoffed at Naomi and continued on her way. If she had, she would have forfeited the blessings of becoming Boaz's wife. In the same way, God's ways sometimes seem a little far-fetched. He wants us to be humble. He wants us to forgive. He wants us to live holy lives. The Holy Spirit helps us understand God's ways, but we must be willing to yield to His guidance. Like Ruth, we must say, "I will do whatever you say."

Cream and Sugar

Is there something about God's ways I really don't understand?

Dear Father, thank you for your Holy Spirit, who helps me understand you. I will do whatever you say. Amen.

Second Cup

For who knows a person's thoughts except their own spirit within them? In the same way no one knows the thoughts of God except the Spirit of God. What we have received is not the spirit of the world, but the Spirit who is from God, so that we may understand what God has freely given us. This is what we speak, not in words taught us by human wisdom but in words taught by the Spirit, explaining spiritual realities with Spirit-taught words. The person without the Spirit does not accept the things that come from the Spirit of God but considers them foolishness, and cannot understand them because they are discerned only through the Spirit. (1 Corinthians 2:11–14)

THE LAST DROP

... stooping very low, He engraves with care
His Name, indelible, upon our dust;
And from the ashes of our self-despair,
Kindles a flame of hope and humble trust.
He seeks no second site on which to build,
But on the old foundation, stone by stone,
Cementing sad experience with grace,
Fashions a stronger temple of His own.

— Patricia St. John

29

POUNDED

God's Word Says

So she went down to the threshing floor and did according to all that her mother-in-law instructed her. (Ruth 3:6 NKJV)

First Cup

Do you know what was done on the threshing floor?

Yes, that's right. Threshing.

Now, to be perfectly honest, I had to look this up. I had a general idea of what threshing was, but I wanted to be sure. To thresh means to strike repeatedly in order to separate the seed from the chaff. In other words, you pound the stuff until you separate the good from the bad, the useful from the useless, the valuable stuff from the garbage. Another form of this word is thrashing. And we all know what it means to receive a thrashing.

Did you notice that in order to get to the threshing floor, Ruth had to go down? Boy, I could write an entire book on that. But the long and short of it is, we are all a little bit like the barley. We have the potential to be useful—to be valuable. But until we spend some time on the Lord's threshing floor, we will have a bunch of useless garbage hanging around our souls.

God wants us to be like Him: loving, kind, compassionate, forgiving, generous, holy. He knows that for most of us to become like Him, we need to have our old sin natures pounded out of us. And before that can happen, we usually have to go down. Far down. To the bottom.

The funny thing is, we all want to have great worth. Yet apart from true saints and lunatics, there isn't one of us who would choose what we have to go through to become godly. There isn't one of us who would say, "Okay, God, pound it out of me! Give me a good thrashing. Just beat me until there's nothing left, so I can be who you want me to be."

Yet I speak from experience. The thrashings—the poundings I've received from this life—really have helped me get rid of a lot of my garbage. The difficult things I've experienced have made me wiser, more loving, and more compassionate. They have made me gentler, kinder, more generous, and more forgiving. I never would have requested the threshing floor. I wouldn't want to do it again, though I'm sure at some point I will. But you know something? I'm glad God loved me enough to see my potential. I'm glad He allowed me to be pounded.

Cream and Sugar

Are there things in my life that I might need to have pounded out of me?

Dear Father, thank you for seeing the value in me and for not discarding me with the chaff. Amen.

Second Cup

Will you have faith in him that he will return your grain and gather it from your threshing floor? (Job 39:12 NASB)

The threshing floors will be full of grain, and the vats will overflow with the new wine and oil. (Joel 2:24 NASB)

For thus says the Lord of hosts, the God of Israel: "The daughter of Babylon is like a threshing floor at the time it is stamped firm; yet in a little while the time of harvest will come for her." (Jeremiah 51:33 NASB)

His winnowing fork is in his hand to thoroughly clear his threshing floor, and to gather the wheat into his barn; but he will burn up the chaff with unquenchable fire. (Luke 3:17 NASB)

THE LAST DROP

If we had no winter, the spring would not be so pleasant: if we did not sometimes taste of adversity, prosperity would not be so welcome.

—Anne Bradstreet

LONG NIGHT

God's Word Says

When Boaz had finished eating and drinking and was in good spirits, he went over to lie down at the far end of the grain pile. Ruth approached quietly, uncovered his feet and lay down. In the middle of the night something startled the man; he turned—and there was a woman was lying at his feet! (Ruth 3:7–8)

First Cup

I can just imagine the pounding of Ruth's heart as she tip-toed over, uncovered Boaz's feet, and lay down. It almost reminds me of one of those secret-agent spy movies, but with a romantic twist. After all, the threshing floor was a public place. All of Boaz's workers, along with their families, slept there. She not only had to avoid waking Boaz; she also didn't want to awaken anyone else either.

I doubt Ruth got much sleep that night. She probably lay there, eyes wide open, wondering how it would all play out.

After all, Ruth's actions likely seemed as strange to her as they do to us. So she lay there, waiting for Boaz to notice her, wondering how he would respond to her.

Sometimes we do the same thing. We lie awake at night, waiting, worrying, wondering how the Master will respond to us. We agonize over this problem or that situation. And during those times, it seems like our Master is sleeping. We wonder when He will ever wake up and notice us. The time of waiting can seem excruciatingly long.

But we don't need to lose sleep. We don't have to waste our time wondering when our Master will notice us. Just as Boaz was in love with Ruth, God is in love with us. He noticed us long ago. He knows our desires. He cares about our problems, and He has already heard the cries of our hearts.

The waiting part is always hard, but Ruth had nothing to worry about. She could have relaxed. She could have rested in knowing that her master was good and loving, and that he would take care of her. And as wonderful as Boaz was, he was nothing compared to our Master.

Are you in a time of waiting? Do you feel like God has fallen asleep? I promise you, He hasn't. He knows. He loves you. Just relax and rest easy. Before long, God will make His presence known. And that, my friend, is worth the wait.

Cream and Sugar

Have I been worried about something? Can I relax, knowing God cares deeply for me?

Dear Father, please help me to be patient. Help me to trust you with every aspect of my life. Amen.

Second Cup

But they who wait for the Lord shall renew their strength; they shall mount up with wings like eagles; they shall run and not be weary; they shall walk and not faint. (Isaiah 40:31 ESV)

I believe that I shall look upon the goodness of the Lord in the land of the living! Wait for the Lord; be strong, and let your heart take courage; wait for the Lord! (Psalm 27:13–14 ESV)

Trust in the Lord with all your heart, and do not lean on your own understanding. In all your ways acknowledge him, and he will make straight your paths. (Proverbs 3:5–6 ESV)

The Lord is good to those who wait for him, to the soul who seeks him. (Lamentations 3:25 ESV)

Be patient, therefore, brothers, until the coming of the Lord. See how the farmer waits for the precious fruit of the earth, being patient about it, until it receives the early and the late rains. You also, be patient. Establish your hearts, for the coming of the Lord is at hand. (James 5:7–8 ESV)

THE LAST DROP

Waiting on God requires the willingness to bear uncertainty, to carry within oneself the unanswered question, lifting the heart to God about it whenever it intrudes upon one's thoughts.

—Elisabeth Elliot

31

SPREAD YOUR WINGS

God's Word Says

The man was surprised late in the night. He turned and saw that a woman was lying at his feet. He said, "Who are you?" She answered, "I am Ruth, your woman servant. Spread your covering over me. For you are of our family." (Ruth 3:8–9 NLV)

First Cup

Have you ever seen a mother hen with her chicks? It's a touching sight, really. I have chickens, and when a mama hen has new chicks, they can disappear right into her feathers. You'd never know they were there. She spreads her wings to provide protection for them at night. She also uses her wings to provide warmth and shelter for them during the day. To those baby birds, their mother is a guardian, a sanctuary, and a source of comfort. As long as they're under her wings, they're safe.

In the ancient Hebrew language, the corners of a garment

were called the wings. So Ruth literally said to Boaz, "Spread your wings over me, for you are my hero, my rescuer." She humbly asked him to take care of her. Like the baby birds, she needed him to provide protection, shelter, and comfort.

But what would happen to one of those chicks if it decided it didn't need to stay under its mother's wings? What if one of the chicks said, "No way, Mama! It's hot and stuffy under there. I feel crowded. I'd rather be out on my own." Yep. We all know the likely ending to that story. The chick would either be ravaged by some wild animal, freeze to death, or, if he came to his senses, he would run back home to Mama as quick as he could.

There is One who wants to protect us. He wants to be our source of comfort, and He wants to shelter us from life's storms. If we stay close to Him, the storms will still come, but He will spread His wings and keep us safe. He will comfort us and keep us warm in His powerful love.

And yes, He will heroically protect us and rescue us from the predator, from the evil one who wants to destroy us. He loves us, and He wants us to stay close to Him, as it's only in the shadow of His wings that we will experience the solace, the shelter, and the sanctuary He longs to give us.

Cream and Sugar

Have I stayed in His shelter? How can I draw closer to His presence?

Dear Father, please cover me with your wings because you are my Rescuer. Keep me close to you. Amen.

Second Cup

He will cover you with His wings. And under His wings you will be safe. He is faithful like a safe-covering and a strong wall. (Psalm 91:4 NLV)

You are my hiding place. You keep me safe from trouble. All around me are your songs of being made free. (Psalm 32:7 NLV)

Keep me as the apple of the eye; hide me in the shadow of Your wings. (Psalm 17:8)

THE LAST DROP

The supreme happiness of life
is the conviction that we are loved.

—Victor Hugo

32

PROVING THEM WRONG

God's Word Says

"The Lord bless you, my daughter," he replied. "This kindness is greater than that which you showed earlier: You have not run after the younger men, whether rich or poor. And now, my daughter, don't be afraid. I will do for you all you ask. All my fellow townsmen know that you are a woman of noble character." (Ruth 3:10–11)

First Cup

When Ruth arrived in Bethlehem, I can just imagine all the gossip that went around town. "Who is that foreign girl with Naomi?"

"She's a pretty little thing."

"Yes, she is. We'd better watch our sons."

"That's true. She'll no doubt set her cap for one of our young men. We can't have that."

"No, we can't. A Moabitess marrying one of our boys? Scandalous!"

Ruth proved them wrong. She wasn't looking for a husband. She didn't use her beauty to try to lure the local boys into marrying her. She was humble, hardworking, and loyal to her mother-in-law. She quietly went about her business, and her actions were always honorable.

You'd better believe people watched her every move. Little by little, they decided maybe she wasn't so bad. Maybe she wasn't such a threat, after all. Maybe, even though she wasn't Jewish by birth, just maybe they would accept her.

When we wear the Christian label, people will watch us. Some people around us will have pre-conceived negative ideas about us. They expect us to be dull. Judgmental. Self-righteous. They watch with suspicion, waiting for us to prove them right.

But when we work hard, when we show humility and not judgment, when we're loyal to our friends and our employers, when we love God and love others and we always try to act honorably, people will notice. They'll say, "Hey, maybe he's not so bad," or "Maybe she's got something we could benefit from." Not only that, but when we behave like Christians should behave, we find favor with our Master. He says to us, "Fear not, for I will take care of you."

Cream and Sugar

Is there someone who has a less-than-stellar opinion of me? What can I do to prove him or her wrong and honor God at the same time?

Dear Father, thank you for Ruth's example of godly

living. Help me to live in a way that honors you and draws others to you. Amen.

Second Cup

Do not let any unwholesome talk come out of your mouths, but only what is helpful for building others up according to their needs, that it may benefit those who listen. (Ephesians 4:29)

A perverse man spreads strife, and a slanderer separates intimate friends. (Proverbs 16:28 NASB)

To malign no one, to be peaceable, gentle, showing every consideration for all men. (Titus 3:2 NASB)

THE LAST DROP

Reputation is what others think of us; character is what God knows of us. When you have spent what feels like eternity trying to repair a few moments of time that destroyed the view others once had of you then you must ask yourself if you have the problem or is it really them? God doesn't make us try so hard, only enemies do.

—Shannon L. Alder

33

A MAN IN LOVE

God's Word Says

"Although it is true that I am a guardian-redeemer of our family, there is another who is more closely related than I. Stay here for the night, and in the morning if he wants to do his duty as your guardian-redeemer, good; let him redeem you. But if he is not willing, as surely as the Lord lives I will do it. Lie here until morning." (Ruth 3:12–13)

First Cup

Well, well! It looks like Mr. Boaz has already done some research. He's a man in love, and he's probably been waiting and waiting for Ruth to give him the signal—the go-ahead. Don't you know his heart leapt when he realized the woman of his dreams loved him back?

But during his wait, he checked things out. He learned there was a closer relative, one who had the right to claim Ruth. Now that he knew she loved him and wanted him to marry her, he needed to work out some details. And like most men in love, he had a plan, but we'll hear about that later.

Right now, though, he's already taken charge as her hero. He knows the highways between his house and Ruth's can be dangerous even in broad daylight. He certainly doesn't want her out alone in the middle of the night. He tells her, "Just stay here and get some sleep. You'll be safe here, and hopefully before we know it, we'll be married. Then I'll take care of you for the rest of your life."

Ruth had a hero who loved her passionately, and so do we. Our Master says to us, "Stay here with me. As long as you remain close, I'll protect you. There's another in this world who wants to claim you, but if I have anything to do with it, he will never touch you! Just relax, lay your problems at my feet, and rest. I'm going to take care of everything."

Have you laid your life at the Master's feet? He has a wonderful plan for you. He wants to love you, care for you, and protect you for all eternity. Like Boaz, He has waited and waited, longing for the moment He would find you at His feet, longing for you to give Him your heart. He wants to be your hero and mine, if we'll only let Him.

Cream and Sugar

Isn't it nice to have a Hero, someone who is madly in love with you and will give His life to protect you?

Dear Father, thank you for loving me passionately. I lay my life at your feet. Amen.

Second Cup

But the Lord is faithful, and he will strengthen you and protect you from the evil one. (2 Thessalonians 3:3)

My God is my rock, in whom I take refuge, my shield and the horn of my salvation. He is my stronghold, my refuge and my savior—from violent people you save me. (2 Samuel 22:3–4)

Do not be afraid, little flock, for your Father has been pleased to give you the kingdom. (Luke 12:32)

THE LAST DROP

He's not your prince charming if he doesn't make sure you know that you're his princess.

—Demi Lovato

34

WHEN MORNING COMES

God's Word Says

So she lay at his feet until morning, but got up before anyone could be recognized; and he said, "Don't let it be known that a woman came to the threshing floor." He also said, "Bring me the shawl you are wearing and hold it out." When she did so, he poured into it six measures of barley and put it on her. Then he went back to town. (Ruth 3:14–15)

First Cup

Have you ever noticed that gossip travels faster than a sonic missile? Not only that, but as it travels, it grows and stretches, and by the time it reaches its final destination, it's turned into something quite different from the truth. Boaz knew this, and he wanted to get to this other kinsman before the gossip did. He wanted to handle this matter quietly and with wisdom. So he told Ruth not to let anyone see her.

Can you just imagine the stories that would have flown

about town, if people had known she claimed Boaz as her kinsman-redeemer? "Why, I thought ol' Joe was a closer relative than Boaz!"

"Yes, I did too. I wonder if Joe knows Boaz is moving in on his territory."

"Beats me. Let's go ask him."

And before you know it, Joe would have been madder than a wet hornet at Boaz, and he would have claimed Ruth as his own simply out of spite.

So Boaz quietly sent Ruth home, but he didn't send her empty-handed. He gave her six measures of barley, which in our terms is about forty-six liters. He gave her more than twice the amount he had given her on the day they met. It was quite a generous gift, and it let her know he was serious about his commitment to her.

I've noticed God's generosity in my own life after I've left the threshing floor. God has always been generous. He's always given me good things. But after going through difficulties, after having had some of the rotten stuff pounded out of my spirit, God has always replaced what's been lost with more blessings than I ever would have thought possible. He replaces the hum-drum with the exciting, the mediocre with the excellent, and the useless things of my life with things that are both fruitful and delicious.

It's as if He's telling me, "Renae, I don't want you to think this visit to the threshing floor was in vain. I love you. I'm committed to taking care of you and providing you with more good things than you can imagine. So here you go. Here's a little taste of what I have in store for you, just so you'll know I'm serious about my love for you."

You may be on the threshing floor right now. You may feel like you're taking a pounding and the night seems so very long. I promise you, morning will come! And when the day breaks, you'll find yourself richer in spirit than you've ever been. Your difficulties won't be in vain as long as you lay yourself at the Master's feet.

Once this season of threshing is over, God will show Himself to you. He'll bless you in a way that will leave no doubt of His enduring commitment and love to you. Hang in there, my friend. The good stuff is on its way.

Cream and Sugar

How has God blessed me after a difficult time in my life? Am I a better person because of the things I've been through?

Dear Father, thank you for your blessings, for your love and commitment to me. I want to commit myself to you during every season of my life. Amen.

Second Cup

Let me hear in the morning of your steadfast love, for in you I trust. Make me know the way I should go, for to you I lift up my soul. (Psalm 143:8 ESV)

O Lord, in the morning you hear my voice; in the morning I prepare a sacrifice for you and watch. (Psalm 5:3 ESV)

For his anger is but for a moment, and his favor is for a lifetime. Weeping may tarry for the night, but joy comes with the morning. (Psalm 30:5 ESV)

The steadfast love of the Lord never ceases; his mercies never come to an end; they are new every morning; great is your faithfulness. (Lamentations 3:22–23 ESV)

THE LAST DROP

When the Japanese mend broken objects, they aggrandize the damage by filling the cracks with gold. They believe that when something's suffered damage and has a history it becomes more beautiful.

—Barbara Bloom

35

REWIND

God's Word Says

When Ruth came to her mother-in-law, Naomi asked, "How did it go, my daughter?" Then she told her everything Boaz had done for her and added, "He gave me these six measures of barley, saying, 'Don't go back to your mother-in-law empty-handed.'" (Ruth 3:16–17)

First Cup

Don't you know Naomi was up all night, pacing the floor, wringing her hands, praying for Ruth? Don't you know she begged God for this scheme to work? After all, it wasn't just Ruth's future at stake. Naomi's future was closely intertwined with Ruth's. Naomi had no heirs, no sons to take care of her. Ruth was her last hope, because if Ruth married and had a son, that son would inherit Naomi's dead husband's land. Naomi's place in the family would then be secured.

So when Ruth returned in the wee morning hours, the

first words out of Naomi's mouth were, "How did it go? Is he going to marry you or not?"

I can just imagine the excited, giddy tone in Ruth's voice as she told the story. This was girl-talk at its best. I mean, seriously. We've got suspense, romance, a hunky hero; it doesn't get much better than this.

But hold on, there's more! Ruth added a bit to the story that was left out before: "Mother dear, Boaz didn't want me to return to you empty-handed. This is for you."

Wait a minute. Press the pause button. This reminds me of something back in chapter one. Hmm, let's rewind, shall we?

Ruth 1:21: "I went away full, but the Lord has brought me back empty."

Now, fast-forward again.

Ruth 3:17: "He gave me these six measures of barley, saying, 'Don't go back to your mother-in-law empty-handed.'"

Now, I want you to rewind and fast-forward as many times as it takes for the light to click on in your mind. Naomi's family left God's Promised Land full and went into the world. She returned empty. Now she was back in God's Promised Land, and she was no longer empty-handed.

Friends, Naomi had it all wrong. It's the world that leaves us empty, not God. Life outside the will of God always robs us, strips us, and leaves us dry as a bone. God is the One who fills us up, who blesses us until we're spilling over. Our Father never, ever leaves us empty-handed. He loves us beyond measure, beyond description. He wants to pour into our lives His riches of wisdom, love, purity, and on and on and on.

When we feel empty, we need to run to our Father and wait at His feet. He loves us, and He wants to fill our lives with His goodness.

Cream and Sugar

How has the world left me empty? How has God filled me up?

Dear Father, help me to recognize your abundance and generosity in my life. Thank you for filling me with your love. Amen.

Second Cup

For in Him all the fullness of Deity dwells in bodily form. (Colossians 2:9 NASB)

And to know the love of Christ which surpasses knowledge, that you may be filled up to all the fullness of God. (Ephesians 3:19 NASB)

THE LAST DROP

Understanding God's love requires not a classroom lecture, but a long bath.

—Dr. Larry Crabb

36

THE WAITING ROOM

God's Word Says

Then Naomi said, "Stay put, my daughter, until you know how the matter turns out. For the man will not rest until he has taken care of the matter today." (Ruth 3:18 NET)

First Cup

Have you ever watched an expectant father pacing about a hospital waiting room? He knows something big, something wonderful is about to happen. And there isn't a thing he can do to influence the course of events. All he can do is wait. All his nervous pacing and nail biting won't make a bit of difference. He might as well just sit down and get some rest.

Easier said than done.

Sometimes we know we're on the brink of something big happening in our lives. Perhaps we're expecting a promotion, or maybe we're waiting on a medical report. We may just sense, somewhere in our spirit, that God is working. But our Master wants us to trust Him with every matter in our lives.

There are some things we just can't control, and no amount of pacing or manipulating or biting our nails will help matters one bit. We must simply have faith that God, who loves us so very much, is going to take care of things. We might as well sit down in our cozy rocking chairs, put our feet up, and relax. Very often, what our Lord wants us to do is wait.

And with the waiting comes trusting. Notice that Naomi said, "The man will not rest until the matter is settled." She had faith in Boaz. She trusted his character, and she knew he'd do all in his power to take care of things.

Our God, who formed us and loves us more than we can imagine, will take care of us. We are His passion! He created us for Himself, because He adores us and wants to have a relationship with us. He's proven His commitment to us again and again, in countless ways. So how can we ever doubt, for a single second, that He is busy seeing to our every need? We don't need to stress ourselves out and worry and fret and chew our nails or eat three pounds of chocolate or whatever it is we do when we're anxious.

We just need to wait. Relax. Rest. Trust His goodness. We can know that our Father, who never sleeps, is always taking care of us.

Cream and Sugar

What am I waiting for right now? Can I relax and trust God to take care of it?

Dear Father, thank you for your constant, everlasting

concern for every detail of my life. Please help me to trust in your love as I wait on you. Amen.

Second Cup

We wait in hope for the Lord; he is our help and our shield. (Psalm 33:20)

Be still before the Lord and wait patiently for him. (Psalm 37:7)

But they who wait for the Lord shall renew their strength; they shall mount up with wings like eagles; they shall run and not be weary; they shall walk and not faint. (Isaiah 40:31 ESV)

The Lord is good to those who wait for him, to the soul who seeks him. (Lamentations 3:25 ESV)

THE LAST DROP

It is very strange that the years teach us patience—that the shorter our time, the greater our capacity for waiting.

—Elizabeth Taylor

37

DOING IT RIGHT

God's Word Says

Boaz went to the city gate and sat there until the close relative he had mentioned passed by. Boaz called to him, "Come here, friend, and sit down." So the man came over and sat down. Boaz gathered ten of the elders of the city and told them, "Sit down here!" So they sat down. (Ruth 4:1–2 NCV)

First Cup

The town gate of that time was kind of like the Starbucks of today. It was the popular hangout. If you were looking for someone and you weren't sure where they'd be, you'd just go wait at the town gate. Sooner or later, the person you wanted would show up. Just like today—sooner or later, that person is gonna need some coffee.

Now, Boaz was a man of high moral character, and he wanted to go about things the right way. He was probably a little nervous. After all, he was in love with Ruth. What if this other guy decided he wanted to marry Ruth? What if Boaz had to stand by and watch the love of his life become some other man's wife—some man who didn't even love her?

Many men in this situation would have just eloped. Then the deed would be done, and even if people whispered about them and looked down on them for the rest of their days, still, it would be worth it, right? At least they'd have each other.

But Boaz wanted better for his bride. She'd already had a hard life. He didn't want to add anything else to the heartache she'd experienced. He loved her enough to risk losing her, in order for her to have the standing in the community that he felt she deserved. So he used wisdom. He did what he needed to do to make her his own, and he did it the right way. He talked to this man publicly and in the presence of respected witnesses. And, as we will soon find out, his integrity paid off.

Very often, when we're faced with situations that might not go the way we want them to, we scheme. We manipulate. We whisper behind closed doors. We make secret phone calls. We call in special favors. We do everything we can to accommodate our cause. Everything, that is, except trust God.

That's not the way God wants His children to operate. He wants us to be above reproach in all things—even when things don't go the way we want them to. He wants us to seek Him and use wisdom and act as He directs. And then He wants us to let go of the situation and let Him handle it. No matter what.

When faced with difficult situations, we can sometimes be tempted to manipulate and scheme in order to bend things in our favor. If we do that, we may win a little battle, but God will not be pleased. And in the long run, the pay-off of living in God's will is much, much greater than doing things our own way.

Cream and Sugar

How can I make sure I'm doing things the right way—God's way—in my current situation?

Dear Father, sometimes it's hard to give up control of things. Please help me to act with wisdom and honor, and to trust you in all things.

Second Cup

But even if you suffer for doing right, you are blessed. (1 Peter 3:14 NCV)

Anyone who knows the right thing to do, but does not do it, is sinning. (James 4:17 NCV)

Let us not lose heart in doing good, for in due time we will reap if we do not grow weary. (Galatians 6:9 NASB)

THE LAST DROP

Knowing what's right doesn't mean much
unless you do what's right.

—Theodore Roosevelt

38

LOVE STORY

God's Word Says

He said to the redeemer, "Naomi, who has come back from the land of Moab, must sell the plot of land belonging to our brother Elimelek. I thought I should inform you and say, 'Buy it in the presence of those sitting here and in the presence of the elders of my people. If you want to redeem it, redeem it. But if you will not redeem it, tell me so that I know, for there is no one prior to you to redeem it, and I am next after you.'" So he said, "I will redeem it." Then Boaz said, "On the day you buy the field from the hand of Naomi, you also acquire Ruth the Moabitess, the wife of the deceased, to perpetuate the name of the deceased through his inheritance." The redeemer replied, "I am not able to redeem it for myself lest I ruin my own inheritance. Take my redemption rights for yourself, for I cannot do it." (Ruth 4:3–6 MEV)

First Cup

This unknown kinsman was very interested in Naomi's land. Notice, he was ready to jump at the chance to purchase it. His head was probably spinning at all the possibilities. He could plant some more crops and make some extra money, and since Naomi had no heirs, the land would stay in his family even at the Year of Jubilee, when all land was returned to the original owner. He was the closest relative. He had a legal right to the land.

But notice how quickly he backed down when he learned he had to marry Ruth as well. In Hebrew culture, it was very important to keep one's bloodline pure. He didn't want to pollute his bloodline by marrying a Moabitess. It would complicate things. So he said, "Never mind."

This kinsman-redeemer represents the one way we can get to heaven without Christ. There is a way, you know. Now, I can hear many of you screaming heresy even as I type. But the truth is, there is a way to get to heaven without Christ, and that is the law. If we can live perfectly under God's laws— if we can live spotless, sinless lives, and if we can remain totally unpolluted by this world and Satan's schemes—then God will welcome us into His heaven.

There's the catch. That little word, *if*. The Bible tells us that all have sinned. Not one of us can be redeemed by the law, because we have all broken God's laws many times over. We have all had impure thoughts, said unkind things, and been disobedient to God. It's our nature to sin—to rebel against God. And so, though the law technically could redeem us, none of us will be redeemed that way. We've all been polluted.

Boaz, on the other hand, represents grace. He adored Ruth. He didn't care that she wasn't Jewish. He didn't care that he would "pollute" his bloodline by marrying her. He just loved her, and he wanted to redeem her—so he did. And Ruth, the Moabitess, was the great-great (many greats) grandmother to our Lord and Savior, Jesus Christ. It was as if God wanted to prove a point by bringing this sweet Gentile woman into His family. His grace is sufficient for all of us. Where the law fails, grace succeeds.

Satan is still trying, to this day, to convince people they have to be perfect. He wants us to believe that if we mess up, we will never be good enough for God, so why bother? He wants us to believe that being perfectly obedient to God's laws is the only way to heaven.

But God knows every detail of our lives. He knows we've been polluted by sin, and He wants us anyway. He has redeemed us simply because He's in love with us. He proved that love by sending His Son to pay the price for our sin. He doesn't expect us to be perfect. He just wants us to love Him back. And the way we prove our love to Him is by living according to His laws—not out of obligation but gratitude.

Have you struggled to be good enough for God? Forget that. It will never happen. Instead, just focus on the love relationship that God wants to have with you. Live your life to please the One who loves you more than anything. Live your life to say thank you to Him. When you mess up, say, "I'm sorry," and then get back on track. When we do this, our relationship with our Redeemer will turn into a beautiful, unending love story.

Cream and Sugar

In what ways have I tried to be good enough for God? Doesn't it feel great to know He loves me even when I'm not perfect?

Dear Father, thank you for your grace, which covers all my inadequacies. I want to live my life as one big thank-you for your love. Amen.

Second Cup

And no creature is hidden from his sight, but all are naked and exposed to the eyes of him to whom we must give account. (Hebrews 4:13 ESV)

For whoever keeps the whole law but fails in one point has become accountable for all of it. (James 2:10 ESV)

You therefore must be perfect, as your heavenly Father is perfect. (Matthew 5:48 ESV)

THE LAST DROP

Nobody's perfect, and our fondest memories of anyone are of the amusing ways they proved it.

—Robert Brault

39

THE SIGNIFICANCE OF SANDALS

God's Word Says

In earlier times in Israel, there was a certain practice. It was used when family land was bought back and changed owners. The practice made the sale final. One person would take his sandal off and give it to the other. That was how people in Israel showed that a business matter had been settled. So the family protector said to Boaz, "Buy it yourself." And he took his sandal off. (Ruth 4:7–8 NIRV)

First Cup

I have recently stumbled upon a darling little blog that focuses on shoes. Having a bit of a shoe fetish myself, I've laughed myself silly over this gal's descriptions of various styles. In it, she recently referred to a men's sandal as a "mandal," and according to her, they should be illegal. But in ancient Israel, apparently mandals were the norm.

In early biblical times, the removal of one's shoes symbolized the giving up of one's power. When Moses approached the burning bush, he removed his shoes. This was an outward symbol of his humility toward God. When a man failed to live up to his responsibility under the law, he would have one or both shoes taken from him in a display of public humiliation.

Here, this unknown kinsman removed his shoe. On the surface, it was a public display of the transfer of his power and rights to the land over to Boaz. He did it willingly in a public declaration. He was saying, "I cannot redeem this land or this widow, but I recognize that you can. Here you go, Boaz. Take it with my blessing. You go ahead and do what I cannot."

Remember, this nameless kinsman represents God's laws. God's laws had the right to redeem us—they were our nearest kinsman so to speak. Yet God's laws, which were intended to keep us holy, have lost their power. Oh, they are still good laws—everything from God is good. But try as we may, we will never be able to live up to them perfectly. So the law has willingly taken second fiddle to another kinsman—One who is both willing and able to redeem us.

Now, what would have happened if Boaz had not been willing to redeem Ruth? Under Jewish law, this other guy would've had to do it. If he refused, then Ruth and Naomi would have been at the mercy of the courts. But Boaz set Ruth free from that other kinsman. And guess what? Jesus Christ has set us free from the law. If not for Christ, the law would be our only hope for salvation. Guess what else? The law would have failed us, and we would have been left without hope.

Many people have asked throughout the ages, "Why did Jesus have to die? What does His death have to do with me?" Well, friends, Jesus had to die because the penalty for sin is death. We couldn't pay that for ourselves because we would have just stayed dead or eternally separated from God in hell. Anyone who perfectly obeyed God's laws wouldn't have to pay that price, but the only One who ever perfectly obeyed God's laws was Jesus. He didn't have to pay the death-price for Himself. He paid it for us.

Now we can go to heaven. It's a free gift—paid in full by our Kinsman-Redeemer, Jesus Christ. He paid the price for our salvation because He is in love with us! And all He asks in return is that we recognize what He did and love Him back. We must simply say, "Yeah, you're right, God. Without Jesus, I would have been left hopeless. Thank you for sending Jesus to pay the price I could never pay for myself."

Cream and Sugar

How can I thank God for what He's done for me?

Dear Father, thank you for loving me enough to pay the ultimate price for me. I love you and want to live for you. Amen.

Second Cup

For what the law was powerless to do because it was weakened by the flesh, God did by sending his own Son in the likeness of sinful flesh to be a sin offering. (Romans 8:3)

Surely he has borne our griefs and carried our sorrows; yet we esteemed him stricken, smitten by God, and afflicted. But he was pierced for our transgressions; he was crushed for our iniquities; upon him was the chastisement that brought us peace, and with his wounds we are healed. All we like sheep have gone astray; we have turned—every one—to his own way; and the Lord has laid on him the iniquity of us all. (Isaiah 53:4–6 ESV)

Greater love has no one than this: to lay down one's life for one's friends. (John 15:13)

THE LAST DROP

Love is that condition in which the happiness of another person is essential to your own.

—Robert A. Heinlein

40

MR. SO-AND-SO

God's Word Says

So the family protector said to Boaz, "Buy it yourself." And he took his sandal off. Then Boaz said to the elders and all the people, "Today you are witnesses. You have seen that I have bought land from Naomi. I have bought all the property that had belonged to Elimelek, Kilion and Mahlon. I've also taken Ruth, who is from Moab, to become my wife. She is Mahlon's widow. I've decided to marry her so the dead man's name will stay with his property. Now his name won't disappear from his family line or from his hometown. Today you are witnesses!" (Ruth 4:8–10 NIRV)

First Cup

Hooray! We got our happy ending. Boaz and Ruth were in love, and now they'd finally be together. Boaz, passionate for his bride-to-be, made a bold declaration in front of all the elders. As a matter of fact, he told the whole town. "I just want everyone here to know, that as of right now, Ruth is mine. She was once known as Ruth the Moabitess. She was once known as Mahlon's widow. But now you can call her Mrs. Boaz!"

I just love fairy-tale endings, don't you? But with every good fairy tale comes a moral to be learned, and this story is no different. The truth of the matter is, though we all wanted Boaz to "win," this unknown kinsman failed. He didn't do his duty. For whatever reason, he was ashamed to marry Ruth—probably because she wasn't Jewish. He was concerned about preserving his own name, his own heritage. He didn't care about preserving Elimelech's name or heritage.

The early Hebrew culture was very concerned about honoring each family by keeping that family's name alive. That's why if a man died without sons to carry on the family name, the closest relative was supposed to marry the widow and provide a son with the dead man's name. This seems strange to us, but it worked for them. It was an important custom.

I find it ironic (and just a tad bit humorous) that this fellow was so concerned about preserving his own name. He didn't want to pollute his family's name or bloodline by mixing it with Moabite blood. That might look bad on the records, but have you noticed what I noticed? We have no clue who this guy was. His name, which was so very precious to him that he wouldn't do his duty to his dead kinsman, is wiped away. Gone! Kaput! Obliterated! This fellow has done a complete disappearing act. As a matter of fact, one translation from the original language calls him "Mr. So-and-So."*

---

* https://enduringword.com/commentary/ruth-4/.

Sometimes we are more concerned about looking good than we are about being good. Sometimes we avoid doing the right thing because we would rather do the politically correct thing. At times, we're more concerned about what people think of us than about what God thinks of us.

Trust me. I've made those mistakes, and even though doing the popular thing may feel good for a season, it won't last. The satisfaction that comes from looking out for number one is temporary. The respect, joy, and peace that come with doing what is right, no matter what, are permanent. If you don't believe me, just ask Mr. So-and-So.

Oh, wait, you can't. We have no idea who he is.

Cream and Sugar

Have I ever been more concerned about doing the popular thing than the right thing? How did it make me feel in the end?

Dear Father, thank you for always acting out of love and always doing what is right. Help me do the right thing, even when it's hard. Amen.

Second Cup

You should want a good name more than you want great riches. To be highly respected is better than having silver or gold. (Proverbs 22:1 NIRV)

The names of those who do right are used in blessings. But the names of those who do wrong will rot. (Proverbs 10:7 NIRV)

A good name is better than fine perfume. People can learn more from mourning when someone dies than from being happy when someone is born. (Ecclesiastes 7:1 NIRV)

THE LAST DROP

Good name in man and woman, dear my lord,
Is the immediate jewel of their souls:
Who steals my purse steals trash; 'tis
something, nothing;
'twas mine, 'tis his, and has been slave to
thousands;
But he that filches from me my good name
Robs me of that which not enriches him,
And makes me poor indeed.

—William Shakespeare, *Othello*

41

BEST WISHES

God's Word Says

And all the people who were at the gate, and the elders, said, "We are witnesses. The Lord make the woman who is coming to your house like Rachel and Leah, the two who built the house of Israel; and may you prosper in Ephrathah and be famous in Bethlehem. May your house be like the house of Perez, whom Tamar bore to Judah, because of the offspring which the Lord will give you from this young woman." (Ruth 4:11–12 NKJV)

First Cup

I was truly blessed the day I met my dear Rick. He is my Boaz. He's strong and handsome, and he loves me in spite of my flaws. I'm not exaggerating when I say I still swoon when he comes near. But many of you may be surprised to learn that he's not my first husband. The reasons for the demise of my first marriage are deeply personal, and I won't belittle God's grace to me by wallowing in the past. But I will say this: I'm not a fan of divorce.

I think our society makes it far too easy to get out of the marriage commitment. Some people—well-meaning people—even secretly root for the demise of our marriages. "He doesn't treat you right," says one friend. "She has really turned into a shrew," says a buddy. The message is clear. Just throw in the towel and start over with somebody new. You can do better.

Here, the elders of Bethlehem rallied around this new couple. They gave their best wishes and their highest expectations. They offered their blessings. They expected nothing less than a successful union.

First, they blessed Ruth: "May the Lord make the woman who is coming into your home like Rachel and Leah, who together built up the house of Israel." Then they blessed Boaz: "May you have standing in Ephrathah and be famous in Bethlehem." Finally, they blessed this family for all their future generations: "Through the offspring the Lord gives you by this young woman, may your family be like that of Perez, whom Tamar bore to Judah."

Friends, we need to protect the sacred union of marriage. Every marriage. We need to pray for, build up, and encourage our friends and loved ones to stay together and make it work. While there are some occasions where divorce is permitted, it should never be desired.

There are some instances when divorce is the right and

just response to a situation—even God Himself gave Israel a certificate of divorce in Jeremiah 3:8. If God is divorced,* and He is without sin, there is clearly a point where divorce is appropriate.

But God hates divorce because He knows how much it hurts. We should hate divorce too, so much that we choose to love our spouses abundantly, excessively, and with sweetness and passion and tenderness and fidelity and acceptance every single day.

Of course, marriage is really a symbol of our relationship to Christ. He loves us perfectly. He sacrificed everything for us. And though we give Him every reason to give up and throw in the towel on us, He never does. He stays there, steady as a rock, always loving, always forgiving, always protecting, always remaining faithful and loyal. He takes care of us even when we don't deserve it. He provides for us even when we forget to say thank you. He is always patient, always kind, always compassionate, and always gentle. He will never ever leave us or forsake us. He will never fail us.

Though I will never love as beautifully or as perfectly as Christ, I will try. For I know the reward of this kind of steady, rock-solid love is beyond measure.

Cream and Sugar

How can I encourage those around me to strengthen their marriages?

---

* For more on this subject, look for *God is Divorced*, by Renae Brumbaugh Green, available as a PDF download at www.ArmoniaPublishing.com.

Dear Father, thank you for the union of marriage. Please help me and our society at large to see the beauty and importance of this sacred institution. Amen.

Second Cup

I gave faithless Israel her certificate of divorce and sent her away because of all her adulteries. Yet I saw that her unfaithful sister Judah had no fear; she also went out and committed adultery. (Jeremiah 3:8)

I will betroth you to me forever; yes, I will betroth you to me in righteousness and in justice, in lovingkindness and in compassion. (Hosea 2:19 NASB)

Marriage is to be held in honor among all, and the marriage bed is to be undefiled; for fornicators and adulterers God will judge. (Hebrews 13:4 NASB)

THE LAST DROP

It is not a lack of love, but a lack of friendship that makes unhappy marriages.

—Friedrich Nietzsche

42

GIFT FROM GOD

God's Word Says

So Boaz took Ruth, and she became his wife, and he went in to her. And the Lord enabled her to conceive, and she gave birth to a son. (Ruth 4:13 NASB)

First Cup

I have two wonderful, beautiful, mischievous, rambunctious, nearly grown children. They fill my heart with joy in a way I never could have imagined before I had them. In my eyes, they are two of the most brilliant, glorious creatures God has ever placed on this earth. And that is how I'm supposed to feel. I am their mother.

What many of you don't know is that one of my children is adopted. I struggled for more than a decade with infertility. The desire for a child is one of the most passionate, most innate, most overwhelming desires I've ever experienced. The inability to conceive left me feeling inadequate, desperate, and broken. When, at fourteen weeks' gestation,

I experienced a miscarriage, I felt totally abandoned and rejected by God. I felt as if He'd played a dirty trick on me—letting me hope and then taking that hope away. It was one of the most difficult things I've lived through.

But now, as I look at my two wonderful children, I know that God was not playing a trick on me. Rather, He was shaping and preparing me for these two special people. He was also preparing me to speak to you today on this very important topic.

Friends, I don't often wade into political waters, and I don't mean to now. But this issue is so close to my heart, and I'd like to respectfully ask you to hear me out on this subject.

Conception is from God. Life begins at conception. And it is a gift. It is a glorious, beautiful gift.

Now, the gifts of a complete family, of a mom and a dad and a stable home—these are gifts parents can give their children either by providing it themselves or by giving up their children for adoption so another family can provide it. And that in itself is something every child deserves.

It doesn't matter if you're thirty-five and married and have been begging God for a child, or if you're fifteen, unmarried, and crossed a boundary that shouldn't have been crossed. It just doesn't matter. Life begins at conception. And life is a gift from almighty God.

It is a most precious gift. Please treat it with the respect and honor that such a gift deserves. Life is a gift from God. And life begins at conception.

Thank you, dear reader, for hearing my heart on this topic.

Cream and Sugar

When is the last time I thanked God for the gift of life?

Dear Father, thank you for the gift of life. Please help me to honor and appreciate that gift. Amen.

Second Cup

Now the word of the Lord came to me, saying, "Before I formed you in the womb I knew you, and before you were born I consecrated you; I have appointed you a prophet to the nations." (Jeremiah 1:4–5 NASB)

People who live on the islands, listen to me. Pay attention, you nations far away. Before I was born the Lord chose me to serve him. Before I was born the Lord spoke my name. … The Lord formed me in my mother's body to be his servant. He wanted me to bring the family of Jacob back to him. He wanted me to gather the people of Israel to himself. The Lord will honor me. My God will give me strength." (Isaiah 49:1, 5 NIRV)

Yet you brought me out of the womb; you made me trust in you, even at my mother's breast. From birth I was cast on you; from my mother's womb you have been my God. (Psalm 22:9–10)

THE LAST DROP

The jewel of the sky is the sun;
the jewel of the house is the child.

—Chinese Proverb

43

MY FAMOUS FATHER

God's Word Says

The women said to Naomi, "We praise the Lord. Today he has provided a family protector for you. May this child become famous all over Israel! He will make your life new again. He'll take care of you when you are old. He's the son of your very own daughter-in-law. She loves you. She is better to you than seven sons." (Ruth 4:14–15 NIRV)

First Cup

This book of the Bible has all the elements of a Hollywood blockbuster movie. It has tragedy, suspense, romance, a beautiful heroine, a handsome hero. As a matter of fact, there is a movie about Ruth.

But of all the players in this drama—Ruth, the leading lady; Boaz, the leading man; and Naomi, the supporting actress—there is one who overshadows them all. He is the One who brought triumph from tragedy. He is the One who took notice of two seemingly insignificant little widows and rescued them. He is the One who took a heart—no, a life—that was shattered in tiny pieces and put it back together in a more beautiful, perfect way than anyone could have imagined.

And yes, He has become famous. His fame has far surpassed Israel; it has traveled to the farthest ends of the earth. He is so famous that His Book is the best-selling book of all time. He is so famous that our historical calendar is measured by the point of His Son's birth. He is so famous that despite persecution and wars that have been fought to squelch His name, His followers have carried on and carried on and carried on. His name is the name above every name.

And one day, at the mention of His name, "every knee should bow, in heaven and on earth and under the earth, and every tongue acknowledge that Jesus Christ is Lord" (Philippians 2:9–11).

We've had famous, powerful kings, but He is the King of Kings. There have been wealthy lords, but He is the Lord of Lords. And I am His daughter. Me. A seemingly insignificant little person. He noticed me. He chose me, adopted me, and made me His own.

And He wants to adopt you too.

Cream and Sugar

Doesn't it feel great knowing my dad is the King of Kings?

Dear Father, I don't know why you, the Creator of all things, the God of the universe, would notice me, but I'm so glad you did. I love you. Amen.

Second Cup

For the Lord is great and greatly to be praised; He is to be feared above all gods. (Psalm 96:4 NKJV)

Yours, O Lord, is the greatness, the power and the glory, the victory and the majesty; for all that is in heaven and in earth is Yours; Yours is the kingdom, O Lord, and You are exalted as head over all. (1 Chronicles 29:11 NKJV)

THE LAST DROP

It is not great men who change the world, but weak men in the hands of a great God.

—Liu Zhenying

44

THE END OF THE STORY

God's Word Says

Naomi took the baby and cuddled him to her breast. And she cared for him as if he were her own. (Ruth 4:16 NLT)

First Cup

As I read this verse, I can't help but remember my two children back before they were nearly grown. There's my daughter: I remember her at ten years old, thin as a rail, a chic fashionista in training and hooked on Nancy Drew mysteries. And my son: Six years old, and at the moment of this memory, bald-headed because he decided to cut his hair. The results were something similar to a reverse mohawk. Lots of hair on the sides. Naked strip right down the middle. He looked like a skunk. After a trip to the barber, he looked like a miniature Kojak.

If I go back even further in my memory, I can almost feel my beautiful little newborn girl. Fat, pink, healthy, wonderful. She was the answer to many prayers and the result of God and infertility treatment.

Four years later, I got pregnant again—the result of many more rounds of infertility treatment. Then, at fourteen weeks gestation, the baby died. I was devastated. I won't even attempt to describe the black hole of depression I entered after that. For the first time in my life, I questioned God's love for me. For the first time in my life, I was so mad at God that I refused to speak to Him.

But have you ever tried to ignore someone who just wouldn't leave you alone? That was my experience with God. He is very persistent. He kept loving me, offering compassion and comfort. And I kept pushing Him away.

He refused to give up. He pursued me, and His constant loving presence finally wore me down. In a moment of tear-drenched surrender, I prayed, *Okay, God. Okay. I don't know what you're doing or why you've allowed me to go through such pain. It makes no sense to me. But okay. I trust you.*

Then came the phone call. A teenage girl we knew was pregnant, and she wanted us to adopt her baby. Within six weeks of my original due date, I held her hand as she gave birth to my son. She held him tenderly, then gave him to me.

Now I can't imagine my life without my two children. I can't imagine being the mother of any other little girl or boy. If I hadn't struggled with infertility, I might not have her. And if I hadn't miscarried, I wouldn't have him. Sure, I might have other children, but it wouldn't be *these* children. And let me tell you, that little girl and that little boy have my heart.

I feel a kinship with Naomi in the moment when she held that baby. She had experienced such great loss. But God gives back. And not only does He give back, but He also always adds something. For Naomi, the grandson she held was the grandfather of the future King David, and a direct ancestor of Jesus Christ. For me, the two children God sent my way have been an endless source of laughter, of deep joy, bubbling over.

Friend, you may be going through a difficult time. You may be experiencing that indescribable black hole that I know so well. Trust me, the end of your story hasn't been composed yet. God never takes away without replenishing. If we'll just trust Him, just surrender to His pursuing, persistent love, we will see miracles. He'll take our sorrow and replace it with giddy joy. He'll take our anger and replace it with peace. Just look at me. He took a barren womb and placed two squealing, squalling, wiggling babies right smack-dab in my arms.

And my story, and yours, is still being written.

Cream and Sugar

How has God surprised me with good things in the past? (There are more surprises to come!)

Dear Father, thank you for the promise of good things in my future. I love you. Amen.

Second Cup

No eye has seen, no ear has heard, and no mind has imagined what God has prepared for those who love him. (1 Corinthians 2:9 NLT)

"For I know the plans I have for you," says the Lord. "They are plans for good and not for disaster, to give you a future and a hope." (Jeremiah 29:11 NLT)

I have told you all this so that you may have peace in me. Here on earth you will have many trials and sorrows. But take heart, because I have overcome the world. (John 16:33 NLT)

THE LAST DROP

Let your hopes, not your hurts,
shape your future.

—Robert H. Schuller

45

THE BIGGER PICTURE

God's Word Says

The neighbor women named him, saying, "A son has been born to Naomi." They named him Obed. Now he became the father of Jesse—David's father! These are the descendants of Perez: Perez was the father of Hezron, Hezron was the father of Ram, Ram was the father of Amminadab, Amminadab was the father of Nachshon, Nachshon was the father of Salmah, Salmon was the father of Boaz, Boaz was the father of Obed, Obed was the father of Jesse, and Jesse was the father of David. (Ruth 4:17–22 NET)

First Cup

Have you ever noticed how self-centered a baby is? Seriously, it's a good thing they're so cute, because if they weren't, they wouldn't stand much of a chance. They cry when they want something. They get angry when they don't get it immediately. They make big messes.

But we adore them! And part of the reason we love them

so much—besides the cute thing—is because we see the bigger picture of their lives. We look at babies and see hope and a future filled with unlimited potential.

I wonder if that's how God sees us. It must be, because honestly, we really don't have much to offer Him. Yet He has the ability to see into the future. He knows what's down the road, and He wants to use our lives as pieces in that road, from the present to the glorious future He has in store for those who love Him. He wants to use us as links in the bridge that leads people to Christ.

Look at Ruth. In many ways, she had a hard life. She was widowed at a young age. She left her family and friends to go into a strange land, expecting to be treated as an outcast and a beggar. I imagine she was thrilled to find Boaz and to have her happy ending. But I'll just bet she didn't have a clue how God wanted to use her in the grand scheme of things. She just quietly lived her life, loving others and loving God. She probably didn't live to see her great-grandson become king. She certainly didn't live to see the Son of God born into her family.

God's plans for our lives are always bigger than our own plans. And very often, He doesn't reveal those plans to us because, truthfully, He knows we would be overwhelmed. If I knew everything God has in store for my children and grandchildren and great-grandchildren, I'd probably try to take the steering wheel away from God and drive things myself.

The future belongs to the Lord. The present, the little

daily choices we make to love others and serve Him—those are ours to make. And when we make them well, when we live our minutes and hours and days for Him, they will always add up to a life that has great significance in the bigger picture.

"And Jacob the father of Joseph, the husband of Mary, and Mary was the mother of Jesus who is called the Messiah. Thus there were fourteen generations in all from Abraham to David, fourteen from David to the exile to Babylon, and fourteen from the exile to the Messiah" (Matthew 1:16–17).

Cream and Sugar

How does God want to use me, today, to be a link in the chain that leads future generations to Christ?

Dear Father, thank you for Ruth's example of humble, gracious, loving service to you and to others. Help me to live each day for you, and to trust you with the future. Amen.

Second Cup

Do not fret when wicked men seem to succeed! Do not envy evildoers! For they will quickly dry up like grass, and wither away like plants. Trust in the Lord and do what is right! Settle in the land and maintain your integrity! Then you will take delight in the Lord, and he will answer your prayers. Commit your future to the Lord! Trust in him, and he will act on your behalf. He will vindicate you in broad daylight, and publicly defend your just cause. (Psalm 37:1–6 NET)

THE LAST DROP

Listen to the mustn'ts, child.
Listen to the don'ts. Listen to the shouldn'ts,
the impossibles, the won'ts. Listen to the
never haves, then listen close to me ...
Anything can happen, child. Anything can be.

— Shel Silverstein

About the Author

This is the place where Renae Brumbaugh Green is supposed to provide impressive things for you to read. But since the most impressive thing about her is the fact that she almost won a car in one of those little fast-food scratch-off games one time, years ago, but she didn't actually scratch off the car until she found the card in her desk drawer long after the deadline had passed … well, there's not much to say.

But if you really want to know about her writing stuff, she's the author of many books, made the ECPA Bestseller list twice, and has contributed to many more books. She's written hundreds of articles for national publications and has won awards for her humor.

She's married to a real hunk, and she's a mom to some amazing kids. She writes music, sings, and likes to perform on stage. She's a sometimes schoolteacher, a part-time chicken farmer, and an all-the-time wannabe superhero. Her favorite color is blue, unless you're talking about nail polish, in which case her favorite color is Bubblegum Pink.

If you want to know more or you'd like to read some of her other books, you can find her at RenaeBrumbaugh.com or check out the Renae Brumbaugh author page on Amazon. com.